5 IN 1

KIRSTIN RAE EVANS

SMALL TALK

BONUS INSIDE

Build Rapport and Network with Ease by Knowing What to Say on Every Occasion

99 TECHNIQUES & INSIGHTS
to Create Powerful Connections by Mastering the
Art of Making Conversation

TABLE OF CONTENTS

INTRODUCTION

As a child, teachers and other adults often told me that I was "an old soul." At the time, I took this as a compliment. Perhaps I was exceedingly wise, I thought, or perhaps they referred to my affinity for reading. I heard other accompanying phrases as I grew older—soft-spoken, shy, wallflower. None of these terms ever bothered me until I started my first job as an adult. Unlike my new coworkers, I was far more reserved and quiet when discussing myself or sharing information. Getting out of my shell and chatting with people seemed insurmountable, and even the idea of initiating conversation was daunting.

All of this will probably sound very familiar to introverts. The nervousness surrounding social interactions can feel isolating, especially if you are introduced to new settings or people. Despite this feeling of being alone, researchers have estimated that over a quarter of the population is introverted. While this may not improve your situation, it is certainly comforting to know that you are not the only one who struggles with the connection. Luckily for us, there is a straightforward way out of this predicament. Communication, as difficult as it may seem now, is a skill; the more you practice speaking to people, the more comfortable you will become with it.

Eventually, I was able to break out of my shell at work. Once I had successful professional conversations behind me, I could apply the same techniques and methods to other areas of my life. In the following books, we will take a deep dive into everything to do with conversations—from walking up to strangers to building rapport, you will be forging meaningful connections before you know it.

You will find 99 techniques, tips, and strategies on how to create powerful connections through making conversation peppered throughout the entire book. It's intentionally designed this way to serve as your guide along each step of the process. This progression is entirely within reach, even for the quietest of introverts.

Book 1: Starting Meaningful Conversations

Beyond Small Talk - Mastering the
Art of Engaging Dialogues for
Deeper Connections

Kirsten Rae Evans

TABLE OF CONTENTS

INTRODUCTION

Unless you are an adrenaline junkie, skydiving probably seems like an uncomfortable, scary, and altogether unpleasant experience. Why do so many people have it on their bucket list? Why do people get into skydiving in the first place?

The answer largely depends on whom you ask. In the words of one skydiving agency, "Whether you have skydived 1 time or 1,000 times, you will know that it does something special to you. Skydiving is a mental game of overcoming fear and battling with your sense of judgment... Skydiving creates confidence" (Skydive Danielson, 2019). Voluntarily throwing yourself out of a moving plane goes against all principles of self-preservation, but it also gives divers a sense of perspective. In short, if you can skydive, you can manage nearly anything that comes your way.

For introverts, starting conversations with strangers may feel like skydiving for the first time. For first-time skydivers and introverts alike, anticipating what is to come is likely the worst part of the activity. However, talking to people like skydiving will likely change your perspective of the world. Once you break out of your initial fear, you might find that life gets significantly easier.

CHAPTER 1

STARTING CONVERSATIONS

E ven with the knowledge, starting to strike up a conversation is hard. Knowing what to say can be tricky at a work gathering or a social party. Mental preparation is necessary before you try to approach someone, and you may also feel better about initiating an interaction if you know what you will say beforehand. With this in mind, let us look at the steps you can take to prepare yourself to interact with a new person.

The Mental Preparation

Before you enter a social situation and walk up to someone, put some mental aids in place. While this process will look different for everyone, all your preparation should center around this fact—*conversation is a skill, and you are learning*. No matter what mistakes you might make on your first couple of tries, and no matter what the outcome is after a conversation, you are simply practicing your socialization skills. No pianist played Paganini perfectly on their first run-through, and no gymnast landed a new flip perfectly on their first try. As with any other acquired skill, the conversation will likely have some awkward twists and turns on your first few tries.

Keeping in line with this idea, try to build habits like:

- **Staying positive.** Worrying about unknown situations is only natural, but worrying does not always serve us. Instead of letting your worries and anxieties run rampant

13

and discourage you from interacting with people, try to keep your emotions on the sunny side of the street. While imagining how a conversation might go may feel unnerving, take a moment to recognize that you do not have all the facts—in other words, you do not have enough information to know how the interaction will go. When preparing yourself, make sure you are going into unfamiliar situations with an open mind, and minimize your worry by visualizing good outcomes.

- **Breathing deeply and relaxing your posture.** Frequently, anxiety causes us to tense up, constricting our muscles and breathing too shallowly physically. While this might make sense if you were skydiving for the first time, this physical stress is inappropriate for socializing. In fact, you have likely noticed that physical stress negatively impacts your ability to focus on mental tasks. In the scenario of initiating a conversation, the same is true. In mentally preparing yourself for socialization, try to breathe deeply and intentionally. According to neurobiologist Andrew Huberman, one of the best ways to slow down and optimize your breathing is by exhaling more than you inhale. One great way to accomplish this is by sighing heavily or inhaling and slowly exhaling through your nose. Your posture is another area that you might need to de-stress, keeping your muscles relaxed.

- **Speak out of curiosity for others.** Now that you know your motivation for conversing with new people, you have probably realized that a lot of that motivation comes from a desire to learn about others. From informational interviews in a particular field to new friends, the biggest aspect of striking up conversations with strangers is a genuine interest in their lives. As you become accustomed to thinking about this, you may find that an authentic curiosity for other people overshadows your anxieties.

For some, the best times to rev up for social interaction are intertwined with previously-existing routines or schedules. For instance, you might prepare yourself to go out and socialize while taking a shower or brushing your teeth in the morning. Additionally, while it might be uncomfortable at first, you should try to put yourself in social situations when possible. Even if you grow too anxious or overwhelmed, you can at least leave the situation knowing you tried. Every effort that you make is a step in the right direction!

Best Ways to Break the Ice

Now that you have mentally prepared to start initiating conversations, it is time to go out there and speak! The scariest part is over for the moment. When you approach someone intending to have a meaningful conversation, however, it is nice to have a couple of good ice-breakers in your back pocket. The ice-breakers you use will depend on your scenario, but questions are a great way to gauge situations.

In more formal, work-related contexts, you will probably want to use ice-breakers that relate to your profession in some way. Additionally, your level of formality depends on whether you are speaking to an authority figure, a peer, or a subordinate. For more general use, questions like *"How is the new project coming along?"* or *"How is your department doing?"* present a great, mild start to a conversation. Inquiring about the general nature of one's work is typically regarded as polite interest, and you will also be able to make inroads with your partner from there. If you are more comfortable with the person you are talking with, or if you are both comfortable talking less formally more specific or challenging questions may be acceptable. That being said, try to keep the content of the questions professional if you are uncomfortable. Queries such as *"Who, or what, was the biggest teacher in your career?"* and *"If you could instantly become an expert in something, what would it be?"* are a little more personal, but they will let you find out more about the person you are speaking with.

In informal contexts, you may be free to use a wider array of potential ice-breakers, depending on how well you know the person. After your initial *"Hi,"* common ice-breakers like *"How are you?"* and *"Where are you from?"* are good candidates for mild conversation. That said, you can always spice things up by catering the question to the person you are speaking to. If you notice that they are wearing a unique or stylish article of clothing, for example, you might break the ice with, *"I love that bag! It looks very stylish!"* or *"Those sneakers look great. Where did you get them?"*. Your surroundings are an awesome way to initiate conversations, so notice things around you. If a particular song is playing, or if you notice a brand or product you have never seen before, ask about it!

Similarly, note how you feel—if you are in a new and fun setting, you might say something like, *"I love this place! Have you been here before?"* or something to that effect. Initially, it is a good idea to stick to things more obvious in a conversation, like the setting or situation around you. Humor may also be a good ice-breaker, but be extremely careful. Everyone's sense of humor is different, and you should only use humor when it fits the situation. When you choose to use humor, make sure that you only talk about basic subjects and do not single out one person or group. Once your partner responds or begins engaging in the conversation, it is best to introduce yourself and tell a little about your background.

Creating a Hook for the Conversation

Let us step back for a moment, and consider what a conversation is at its most elementary level—an exchange of information between two people. Talking with a new person is an informational exchange that you and a stranger perform for as long as the conversation lasts. As a result, the things you convey determine the impression you make and the potential relationship you will have with this person going forward. Before you start talking to people, it is a good choice to have a general idea of what you want to say to make a good impression.

Think back to your last truly engaging or interesting conversation—*what was it about?* While making small talk is fine for the first few minutes of a conversation, choosing a specific subject, theme, or topic is crucial in turning a simple exchange of words into a meaningful conversation. Here, we will call the things you choose to discuss the hook of your conversation.

While you might not always discuss your hook directly, this is the theme you will be revolving around throughout the conversation. Broad hooks like your current setting, school, and work are all common, and these are all good places to start if you are still uncomfortable conversing with strangers. Some of the most engaging hooks happen when the focus is deeper, especially when they pertain to more personal wants or needs. Speaking openly and honestly about your aspirations, hopes, and anxieties will likely make your conversational partners do the same, creating more meaningful conversations. Suddenly, simple how-are-you's turn into a deep discussion about successes, struggles, and commonalities.

Now that you know about hooks, it is important to note that conversation is not an exact science. It may take some twists and turns, and you might find the conversation ending in a completely different place than where it started. If you let go of your initial hook after a while, do not worry—this may be a sign of a good conversation! Additionally, it takes two to make good conversation. Speaking about yourself is great, but you should also actively listen to the person you are talking to. Keep an ear out for good points or sentiments that you agree with. If your conversational partner says something interesting, try the three-second rule. The three-second rule entails sitting silently for at least three seconds before trying to respond to your partner, and this method may improve the quality of the conversation you are having.

All in all, you will likely find that conversation is far easier once you have made the initial jump. Starting a conversation with a stranger can be scary, even for self-proclaimed extroverts. With enough mental preparation, ice-breakers, and situational awareness, however, you will begin to feel much better about initiating conversations in the future.

CHAPTER 2

TONE AND INTENTION

Once you have entered a conversation, you do not want to ruin a conversation by using the wrong tone or delivery once you have entered it. Despite being a simple exchange of information between two parties, the conversation can be deceptively tricky at times, both in personal and professional interactions. According to business communications expert Dave Richards, "Tone of voice, pauses in conversation, and the presence or absence of social 'niceties' can shape customer experience more than the actual service provided. A delay in follow-up, noncommunication, may result in a loss of opportunity" (Richards, 2014). The difference between an advance in your career and a lost opportunity may rest entirely on the tone of your voice. Similarly, personal and social relationships are also fraught with tonal pitfalls. For instance, the use of humor or sarcasm with a new acquaintance can easily be mistaken for rudeness.

For introverts, navigating tone in conversation can be even more challenging. Speaking quietly or not speaking at all can easily lead to misunderstandings, especially when meeting new people. To avoid this, understand your motivation for socializing, speaking to your conversational partner with clear intentions.

Speaking With Intention

In the last chapter, we talked about understanding your motives and emotions before you enter a conversation with someone. Motives can range from making new friends to opening new career opportunities, but you should understand how your motive is unique to you. The more specific you can determine your motivations, the more accurately you can express them to others. In this way, your motivation for socializing will function as an overarching goal for all your conversations. Sometimes, writing down a short descriptive statement on a sticky note can help clarify your motivation/goal for communicating with people. No matter what your goal statement looks like, you should generally try to follow the guidelines of a SMART goal or a specific, measurable, attainable, realistic, and timely goal. A good goal statement might look something like:

- *"I want to make at least three new friends by the end of the year."*
- *"I want to network with at least ten new professionals in my field in the next month."*
- *"I want to build at least five new client relationships by the end of the quarter."*

Notice that each statement includes a numerical metric and a clear time frame. This will help keep you accountable throughout your conversations and give you a specific number or deadline to aim for. The above statements are great starters, but do not be afraid to go further—the more specific you can make your statement, the more you will understand your goals. Think back to your goal statement when you begin talking with folks, whether personally, professionally, or otherwise. Your motivation/goal statement should correlate with the conversational hooks you use.

Let us take an example—Say you have just moved to a new city, and your goal is to meet at least three new people in your first week there. Your hook should include some of that information when you start interacting with people. This might look like:

- *"Do you know any good coffee shops around here? I am new to the area."*
- *"Can you help me find ____? I have never been to this city before."*

- *"This is such a cool store! They do not have these where I am from."*

These are all great hooks that will give your conversational partner some insight into your intentions for socializing.

But why does clarifying your goals and motivations matter in the first place? Can you not just talk with a stranger and see where it leads? While this approach may work for some, introverts may find this difficult. Not seasoned conversationalists may hit snags in their interactions, especially regarding delivery and saying what you mean. Often, making your intentions clear from the outset of interaction greatly minimizes the chance of miscommunication. As one Westfield State College study states, *"For effective communication to occur, conversationalists must agree on the intention of the message; otherwise, the conversation may evolve in a way that was not predicated on the speaker's message (from the speaker's perspective)."* In other words, conversations with clear intentions have less chance of going off-course, allowing you to socialize effectively and efficiently. Furthermore, if your conversational partner sees you as honest and authentic, they are likelier to continue talking to you.

Using the Right Tone

Another important aspect of good conversations is tone and affect delivery. Chances are, you have likely encountered miscommunications through asynchronous formats, like email or text. This is largely because you cannot see your partner's face, body language, or delivery, so some messages may sound different from what your partner intends. Strangely, the same thing can happen in person, especially for those uncomfortable or experienced in conversation. When you feel anxious or nervous about talking to people, you are often too distracted to notice the qualities of your voice or facial expressions. This can often lead to dissonance between what you mean and what you say, leading your conversational partner down a different path than the one you have in mind. In short—an introvert's worst nightmare.

To combat this, you should work to gain better control over the tone you use. First, let us define tone: According to voice coach Maria Pellicano, *"Tone of voice is the non-verbal aspect of speaking. The tone is [vocal] intonation…[and] inflection, which is the sound's rise and fall. It may also be a vowel in the syllable of the word sustained or an over-pronounced consonant."* As you likely know, different tones have different meanings, and good conversations largely depend on maintaining an interested, optimistic, and engaged tone while speaking to your partner.

Researchers in communications and psychology have grappled with tonal quality for decades, and various metrics and categorization systems have arisen. Nielsen Norman Group, a user experience consulting firm, describes one method of analyzing vocal tone with a four-dimensional model; funny versus serious, formal versus casual, respectful versus irreverent, and enthusiastic versus matter-of-fact. For instance, a serious and irreverent tone is often perceived as snarky or sarcastic, whereas a casual and enthusiastic tone is perceived as friendly.

Before you begin initiating conversations, consider that your tone is affected by your motivations, emotional state, and the setting you are in. If you feel anxious, your tone will reflect that to your partner. Similarly, if you are in a loud, stimulating setting, you will have more trouble adjusting your tone to fit the situation. Reflect also on your goal statement—with detailed knowledge of yourself, your motivations, and your unique situation; you are closer to recognizing the tone that will accomplish your goals. Going back to the example of making friends in a new city, the best tone to use will be funny, casual, respectful, and enthusiastic, according to the four-dimensional model. To get this tone across to your conversational partner, you would want to speak with an even inflection, making sure to breathe deeply and smile as you talk. When having your first conversation with a new person, speaking slightly slower and softer than you normally would is also best. That being said, you never want to mumble or talk in a mono-tone way, as this usually indicates that you are not interested in continuing the conversation. While it might seem strange initially, recording yourself or practicing speaking in a mirror is a great way to gauge your tone and facial expressions.

Managing your tone can be a tricky skill to master. However, with enough real-world practice and self-awareness, you can control your vocal tone quickly. Now that you know how to get your message across in a conversation, let us dive into how to keep your partner engaged. In the next chapter, we will review the power of questions, how to use them, and how to ask good questions.

CHAPTER 3

QUESTIONS IN A CONVERSATION

At some point, we have all been caught in boring conversations we do not want to be in. Unfortunately, from school to work to social gatherings, there are always opportunities for bad conversation. Normally, we want to avoid situations like these entirely or, at the very least, escape quickly. If this sounds like you, you are certainly not alone! One Harvard study examined 932 different two-people conversations between strangers, with the conversations lasting for 45 minutes. Of the 932 pairs, 50% of participants wanted their conversations to end far sooner. Since introverts comprise only 25% to 40% of the population, introverted folks are not the only people with communication problems.

So, why are so many conversations so difficult to sit through? Aside from ice-breakers and tone issues that we have already discussed, there is yet another pitfall when making conversation—engagement issues. Sometimes, the person you are talking with simply is not saying much. For conversationalists, this is one of the worst things that can happen, often fizzling the conversation. If you are familiar with the subject, you might know the term "nonversation" or something similar. On the other end of the spectrum, *you* might be the unengaged partner in a conversation, waiting for your chance to run to the exit. Alternatively, you and your conversational partner may feel that there is nothing more to say, resulting in an awkward conclusion. No matter which of these scenarios happens, these types of conversations are not what we are looking for when we want to have long-term, meaningful interactions.

Poor engagement can be a major barrier for those looking to build up their conversational skills. You do not want to be the only one talking in a conversation or be on the receiving end of a rambling lecture. Luckily, poor engagement issues can be solved with one simple strategy—asking questions.

Why Ask Questions?

Remember the last time you were caught up in a bad conversation? Likely, the conversation started normally, with mutual greetings, a couple of basic questions, and then… The balance of exchange fell away. Whether you found yourself in a one-sided conversation or an awkward silence, there was a point where you had stopped communicating effectively. In other words, there was an interruption to the flow of information somewhere along the way.

We ask questions in the hopes of receiving information all the time, from a Google search to a team meeting at work. When information is lacking, asking questions is the first thing we should do. The same can be said of socialization. You will get great results when you pair honesty and authenticity with a good question.

To get a better sense of what this might look like in practice, let us take a few examples:

1. **Awkward beginnings.** An all-too-common occurrence for introverts, awkward starts can be deeply uncomfortable. These conversations usually start something like this:

    PERSON 1: HI! HOW'S IT GOING?

    PERSON 2: I AM GOOD. WHAT ABOUT YOU?

PERSON 1: I AM DOING PRETTY WELL.

Followed by silence. Usually, people in these types of conversations are open to talking further but do not know how to maintain engagement. Typical, run-of-the-mill questions lead to typical answers, and before you know it, you have run out of things to say. However, using a simple question catered to the situation can spice up these awkward beginnings:

PERSON 1: HI! HOW'S IT GOING?

PERSON 2: I AM GOOD. WHAT ABOUT YOU?

PERSON 1: I AM DOING ALL RIGHT. I JUST MOVED INTO MY NEW APARTMENT YESTERDAY. DO YOU HAPPEN TO KNOW OF ANY GOOD USED BOOKSTORES AROUND HERE?

PERSON 2: YEAH, THERE IS A GREAT ONE A COUPLE OF BLOCKS FROM HERE, ACROSS FROM THE POST OFFICE. LOOKING FOR ANYTHING IN PARTIC-ULAR?

PERSON 1: I NEED A COUPLE OF BOOKS FOR A CLASS I AM TAKING; I AM A PSYCHOLOGY MAJOR.

PERSON 2: WOW, THAT IS SO COOL! DO YOU LIKE YOUR CLASSES SO FAR?

In this situation, you can see more engagement from both parties. Information is being exchanged equally, and both people are asking questions. As a result of the exchanged questions and answers, there is more information to build off. This conversation could discuss school, psychological concepts, cool bookstores in the area, and much more. Comparatively, the pair in this situation are far more likely to become friends or acquaintances than in the first situation.

2. **A one-sided conversation against you.** If you are anything like me, it usually takes more effort for you to speak in a conversation. It can be easy for your social battery to get drained in conversations with strangers, especially if you are not used to socializing regularly. As a result, some conversational partners take this opportunity to spend the entire conversation talking, leaving you with no chance to get a word in edgewise. Aside from being a boring and unengaging way of communicating, it can also be difficult to escape these situations.

   Enter: Asking good questions. While you might not see any opportunities initially, your conversational partner will inevitably need to take a breath, bite food, or pause their monologue. In these moments, a good question can redirect the conversation, changing the subject or evoking a longer pause from your partner. This situation may go a little something like this:

   > PERSON 1: ...AND THAT IS WHY I DO NOT LIKE USING PLASTIC BAGS AT THE STORE.
   >
   > PERSON 1: ...
   >
   > PERSON 2: WHEN MUST YOU RETURN TO THE OFFICE TODAY?
   >
   > PERSON 1: AROUND NOON, I THINK.

PERSON 2: I THINK I WILL GROCERY SHOP BEFORE I HEAD HOME. DO YOU MIND IF I DUCK OUT?

PERSON 1: NO, NOT AT ALL! SEE YOU LATER!

Here, Person 2 uses questions to gain more information about leaving the conversation. By bringing up a time-based limitation, the tone of the conversation changes, and Person 1 no longer has an opportunity to ramble. Rather than simply sitting through more rambling, Person 2 has determined a polite way of exiting the conversation without offending the other person.

3. **A shallow conversation.** Perhaps the most common type of conversation associated with small talk is shallow conversations that stay at surface level. We have all been there—you start a conversation with a new person, and all you can talk about is the menial, boring, tedious stuff in your immediate vicinity. This type of interaction gets tiring for both parties quickly, and the conversation usually stops within a few minutes. For introverts and those who do not like socializing, this is perhaps the most dreaded scenario imaginable. However, as you might have picked up, shallow conversations remain at surface-level subjects because of a lack of information. Often, we do not have any interesting information to build on, making the inter-action seem dry and meaningless. In this instance, a good and thought-provoking question can immediately result in better engagement from your partner (and a potential new friend or acquaintance). Let us look at an example between two coworkers who have just met recently:

COWORKER 1: HEY, HOW IS IT GOING?

COWORKER 2: GREAT! HOW ABOUT YOU?

COWORKER 1: GOOD, I AM JUST WORKING ON SOME ADMINISTRATIVE STUFF.

COWORKER 2: YES, THAT NEW SOFTWARE WILL TAKE SOME TIME.

At this point, the conversation could go one of two ways—either both parties continue talking about menial workplace tasks and complaints, or someone asks a good question to reset the tone and subject of the conversation. The question could concern anything if it is relevant and more interesting than the current subject. In this case, the presentation of a good question could go something like this:

COWORKER 1: HEY, ARE YOU INTO SUPERHERO MOVIES?

COWORKER 2: YES! A NEW ONE JUST CAME OUT; I AM SEEING IT ON SATURDAY. I AM SUPER EXCITED!

COWORKER 1: SAME HERE! I HOPE IT IS BETTER THAN THE LAST ONE.

COWORKER 2: ME TOO, THE LAST BIG SUPERHERO MOVIE I SAW WAS NOT THAT GOOD...

At this point, both parties are engaged in discussing a relevant and more interesting topic than work.

How to Ask the Right Questions

Good questions can take many forms, from hobbies to goals and aspirations. While the types of questions you ask depend on the context of your conversation, good questions should have three core characteristics:

- Genuine curiosity
- Authenticity
- Respect

If you are authentic, respectful, and curious about the subject of your question, you will find that conversation becomes a lot easier. Not all the questions you ask will have the same efficacy. Some questions will yield better results than others, namely those that take the information you have learned about your partner and build on it. According to one Harvard researcher, conversational questions can be divided into four general groups; **introductory questions** *(the initial "How are you doing today?")*, **mirror questions** *("I am doing well, and you?")*, **full-switch questions** *(questions that change the subject of the discussion)*, and **follow-ups** *(questions that use existing information to attain more)*. Of these four, follow-ups are the most effective when diving deep into a particular topic.

Imagine for a minute conversing with a new person. If your conversational partner *only* asks you yes-or-no questions, you might begin to feel as if you are being interrogated. From the perspective of attaining new information, straightforward yes-or-no questions leave little room for elaboration or explanation. Yes-or-nos are generally better for professional situations that require direct responses or answers that are straight to the point. For some, this type of questioning can convey a sense of urgency or tenseness, which is not conducive to forming new connections. Open-ended questions best suit more casual or normal personal or professional conversations.

The order in which you ask questions is as important as the questions you ask. If you go up to a stranger and ask a very deep or personal question *(think, "Have you ever cheated on your partner?" or "What is your biggest regret in life?"),* you will likely receive negative responses. These questions come off as abrasive and brazen when you do not have a relationship with someone. Instead, more surface-level questions are a better option for relationship-building. Researchers suggest that people looking to form good social or professional connections start with least-intrusive questions first and then slowly build to more personal questions over time.

Additionally, you should ask questions frequently throughout your interactions, not just once or twice. In addition to taking the impetus off yourself, this will make your conversational partner feel valued, listened to, and interested.

While it is important to remember all this information, it is sometimes better to lean on some good, ground-level questions. This might look like:

- Did you choose your profession, or did it choose you?
- How did you decide to go into this field?
- How long have you been in your field?
- What is your favorite part of your job?
- What is the most challenging part of your job?

All these generally work well. If your conversational partner responds to questions like these with good information, asking follow-up questions about their response is a surefire way to start building a good professional relationship. After a while, you may find that different variations of these questions work better for you. Try to make your questions personable, authentic, respectful, and genuinely curious.

Meanwhile, more casual conversations will be better suited by questions like:

- What is the last good movie/show you watched?
- What kind of music do you listen to?
- What do you like to do when you are not working?
- Where would you go if you could go anywhere in the world for free?
- Do you think you have survived the zombie apocalypse?
- Are you into podcasts at all?
- If you had to choose, are you more of an introvert or an extrovert?
- What is the craziest thing on your bucket list?

Or something similar. While you might have more leeway regarding subjects in casual conversation, remember to always respect your conversational partner. If you do not know your partner well, try to avoid the standard party-killer topics like politics and religion.

Using Questions to Dodge the Awkward Turns

Unfortunately, there are awkward moments in almost all conversations, even for the best of conversationalists. This awkwardness is part of interacting with people, from lulls to lacking responses. You will not always have smooth, flowing conversations, which is perfectly normal. If you are not rambling, pestering your conversational partner, or using the wrong tone, you have nothing to worry about.

Even still, awkwardness in conversation can be uncomfortable for you and your partner. Good conversationalists know how to get around these awkward turns. For beginners, the best way to do this is with questions. Awkward turns can happen for various reasons, but it can be especially painful when you have run out of information for your follow-up questions. At this point, you can essentially regard these lulls as dead ends—in other words, you have explored everything you can explore with this topic, and it is time to change things up. The full-switch questions we talked about earlier come in handy in these cases. Full-switch questions can sometimes be difficult if you are already conversing with someone, so they require a bit of thought and effort. Typically, good full switches are somehow connected to the previous topic of conversation, simply redirected down another road. Let us take an example to see how this might work. Two new acquaintances are having a conversation, but they have hit a lull after discussing their favorite TV shows:

PERSON 1: ...AND THAT IS WHY I LOVE SUPER-HERO SHOWS.

...

PERSON 2: IT SOUNDS LIKE YOU ARE PASSIONATE ABOUT THE GENRE. HAVE YOU EVER TRIED WRITING A SUPERHERO SHOW YOURSELF?

PERSON 1: NO, I AM NOT A GREAT WRITER. I JUST DO NOT HAVE THE KNACK FOR DIALOGUE. HOW ABOUT YOU, DO YOU LIKE WRITING?

PERSON 2: I LOVE WRITING! I SUBMITTED A SHORT STORY TO A WRITING COMPETITION LAST MONTH.

PERSON 1: REALLY! THAT IS SO COOL! WHAT WAS THE STORY ABOUT?

The conversation between these two people went from super-hero shows to creative writing. *But how?* Person 2's question, *"Have you ever tried writing a superhero show?"* effectively linked two ideas, bridging one subject and another. This is a great pivot when conversations start to dry up, and it works especially well when you connect similar subjects. In this case, superhero shows and writing might be connected through a broad category like arts or entertainment, making the bridge more manageable for both parties.

In conjunction with pivoting questions like this, it may also help to be honest about what is happening in the conversation. Acknowledging the awkwardness can be a refreshing way of interacting and can also help ease tensions and anxieties in your partner. Let us look at the same scenario in which Person 2 uses this method:

PERSON 1: ...AND THAT IS WHY I LOVE SUPERHERO SHOWS.

...

PERSON 2: WOW, I THINK WE HAVE COVERED ALL THERE IS TO COVER ABOUT SUPERHEROES! THE PRODUCTION STUDIOS SHOULD HIRE US AS CONSULTANTS.

PERSON 1: I HAD LOVE TO WORK FOR A TV STUDIO; THAT WOULD BE SO COOL! IT WOULD BE AWESOME TO BE AROUND OTHER ARTISTS ALL THE TIME.

PERSON 2: DOES YOUR DREAM JOB INVOLVE ALWAYS WORKING AROUND ARTISTS?

Again, the conversation between these two people went from superhero shows to a similar topic, TV production. Person 2 successfully pivoted by acknowledging the awkwardness and adding comments, and when they received more information from their partner, they could ask a follow-up question. This honesty and authenticity ultimately continued the conversation and kept the two people engaged.

Now, you understand the basics of conversation, including icebreakers, conversational hooks, and asking good questions. While this is a great base for interacting with strangers, there is always more to learn when socializing. Next, we will tackle the obstacle of first impressions and how to stand out to the people you meet.

Book 2: Psychology of Initial Encounters

First Impressions Unveiled - Deciphering the
Mind's Landscape in New Meetings

Kirsten Rae Evans

TABLE OF CONTENTS

INTRODUCTION

We have all heard the adage—do not judge a book by its cover. In reality, we tend to judge many things based on appearance. Everything—from what brand of milk you buy at the supermarket to which people you decide to speak to—is based on how things look. There is more to these choices than simply visual appearance. All our sensory information can be used to make snap judgments. When we encounter new information, objects, and people, our determinations can be based on anything. Smell, touch, and sound are just as important as sight, and we regularly use all these tools to make decisions.

Would you opt to talk to someone with bad breath? Would you interview a job candidate who looks like they have just rolled out of bed? Would you feel comfortable around someone who does not respect your personal space or someone who yells when they speak? Chances are, you prefer to converse with people you feel make a good impression. Inversely, you should prioritize your first impressions if you want to find success in your conversations.

CHAPTER 1

MEMORABLE FIRST IMPRESSIONS

W e all know that first impressions are important on some level, but why exactly do they matter so much?

To find an answer, let us look at food as an example. Think about a type of food you did not like in your childhood—I always hated Brussels sprouts. Whatever your least favorite food was as a kid, you probably developed that preference the first time you tried the food. All it took was one taste, and you suddenly reacted negatively to the experience. Eventually, I overcame my disdain for Brussels sprouts, as many people develop different tastes as they age. However, our tastes in childhood often last for years *(occasionally even into adulthood)*, often as a direct result of a childhood experience. Unfortunately, the same can be said of many different things in life, from movie genres to roller coasters. When you meet someone for the first time, the first few minutes of speaking can have a long-lasting effect on how you are perceived.

The Mind and First Impressions

This long-lasting effect has a name in psychology—the first impression bias. While the question of how this tendency developed in humans is debated, there is an overwhelming consensus that this first impression bias is extremely common amongst all demographics. As much as we do not like to admit it, we are all guilty of judging books by their covers! According to research firm The Decision Lab, first impressions can take as little as 0.1 of a second to form. To make matters even more nerve-wracking for novice conversationalists, the accuracy of first impressions is still much debated in the scientific community. Even for the most confident conversationalists, this can breed fear and anxiety around looking, sounding, and acting your best. In turn, the pressure from this knowledge can make us hyper-aware of ourselves in social situations, compounding the problem and making us even more nervous in front of new people.

Before you lock yourself in your room forever, do not worry! It is not all doom and gloom when it comes to first impressions. According to one BBC article, a huge segment of people thinks they have poor conversational abilities and their social first impressions. Furthermore, this feeling toward ourselves mani-fests in something called "the liking gap," or the gap between how poorly we think of ourselves in social situations and how highly others think of us. This liking gap can persist for several months when we meet and interact with new people, or at least until we have formed solid relationships. This gap can wreak havoc on our ability to interact, and our self-doubt can inhibit our ability to form meaningful connections.

Luckily, there is one good thing we can draw out of this data—first impressions certainly matter, but you are also probably underesti-mating how much people like you. Before initiating conversations, it is important to take some time to mentally prepare and ground yourself. While you may be a little rusty with your social skills, remember that strangers will likely form good impressions of you if you make a concerted effort.

Making a Positive Lasting Impression

As you likely know, making good impressions is not just about how you speak. Your body language, tone of voice, clothing, and facial features all affect how people perceive you, especially when you have just met. While you cannot exactly change things like your facial features, accents, or physical appearance, there are aspects of your presentation that you can control, like clothing choices, tone of voice, and body language. These factors should be catered to the context of your conversations, but you should generally always put effort into your appearance and hygiene. Having properly-fitting clothes, an open and lighthearted tone of voice, and a good attitude is a great place to start when making a good first impression.

Aside from basics like good hygiene, there are even more things you can do to boost your first impression from the perspective of your conversational partners, such as:

- **Maintaining good eye contact and a positive facial expression.** For some, making direct eye contact during conversation can be difficult. This practice can vary by culture, but Americans tend to interpret direct eye contact as interest in the conversation. If you plan to interact with Americans, try maintaining eye contact with your conversational partner while they are speaking. If you plan on interacting with people from different cultures, try to learn more about that culture's perception of good manners. Almost every culture in the world recognizes the importance of a good smile. Smiling regularly when you speak is a great way to show your partners that you care about the conversation.

- **Speaking calmly and confidently.** Sometimes, nervousness and anxiety present through fast, hurried speech. If you have ever been on the receiving end of this kind of conversation, you know it is not an ideal way to start a conversation. Rather than trying to get your points across as quickly as possible, try slowing down the speed of your speech. Doing so will also decrease the likelihood of stumbling over your words, making the interaction much smoother. When you talk, try pausing every so often for about two or three seconds to ensure your partner has opportunities to jump in.

- **Keeping good posture.** Posture and body language are things that you do not notice until you are in front of a mirror. Unfortunately, one of the scariest parts of meeting someone for the first time is that you do not know what you look like in their eyes! However, good posture and open body language always convey openness and interest. Standing straight back, relaxed, and shoulders lowering is a great starting point in all situations. Additionally, you should try not to cross your arms, hang your hands in your pockets, or slouch your shoulders, as this can sometimes make you seem untrustworthy or bored.

These are all actions that you can take to put your best foot forward, both in casual and professional settings.

Using the Right Vocabulary

Here is where things get a little trickier—the words you use in conversation can make or break a first impression, and your words must be catered to the situation. To make things easier to remember, we will break down vernacular into three categories. Professional language is a language that you use strictly in professional situations, regardless of industry or partner. Commercial language is vocabulary that you use in situations where you are selling a point, product, or idea. Finally, social language is a language that you will use in everyday conversations with strangers outside of work. All three are very different, and knowing how to get your message across in conversations in these three contexts is important.

Professional Language

No matter your field of work, the language you use at work should differ noticeably from the language you use at home or with friends. Part of this is because of the context of your conversations; You might find yourself speaking with people who outrank you or in gatherings that only concern professional matters. The other part of this equation is the lack of familiarity with your conversational partners. Chances are, you probably do not know everyone at your place of work unless you work in a small business. As a result, you do not know people's sense of humor, boundaries, or expectations when having professional conversations. These factors, unfamiliarity, and context, require you to use broad, general language. Things like humor, sarcasm, or niche references that you might use in conversations with friends or family are unsuitable for professional conversations. If this is the first time speaking to a professional in your field, you should keep the three Cs in mind—you want to be calm, confident, and competent. In other words, you want to make yourself seem like the best version of yourself. This is especially true for networking events or interviews, where the next phase in your career depends on how you present yourself.

Before you enter professional situations like a new job, an interview, or a networking event, try drawing up a list of everything you want strangers to know about you. This list can have anything from soft skills, like responsibility or strong communication skills, to hard skills, like knowing program languages or having a unique knowledge of something in your field. After making your list, think about words you could use to convey these things to people in professional conversations.

For instance, here are some words that you could use to describe accomplishments:

- Negotiated
- Supervised
- Coordinated
- Managed
- Pioneered

If you work in a specialized industry, it is a good idea to look at job postings on platforms like Indeed or LinkedIn *(even if you are not looking for a job)*. Job descriptions in your industry will give you a great idea of what people in your field sound like when they speak professionally. In each job posting, keep an eye out for words that you could use that are industry-specific.

However, you do not want all your conversations to center around metrics or hard skills. Soft skills are just important, and you also want to show professionals in your field that you understand the culture of your work. According to one finding from Forbes, a survey of over 500 executives in multiple industries discovered that emotional intelligence (EQ or soft skills) better predicted future success than one's resume or accomplishments. Similarly, a survey of 200 companies found that EQ was nearly twice as important as hard skills when ranking employee importance. So, before diving into the technical terminology world, remember to incorporate some soft-skill jargon into your conversations. Here are some great options for emphasizing your EQ:

- Consistent
- Trustworthy
- Punctual
- Responsible
- Passionate
- Optimistic
- Open-minded
- Respectful
- Committed

The Dangers of Jargon

Now, you might think that you are ready to go out and network in a professional setting. However, there is one thing that you should always keep an eye on when you are speaking to people. Jargon is often a double-edged sword; on the one hand, it allows you to show your competence in a particular field. On the other hand, using too much jargon can also weigh down your conversations and make them unintelligible. According to the U.S. Plain Language Action and Information Network, "Going beyond necessary technical terms to write in jargon can cause misunderstanding or alienation, even if your only readers are specialists." In writing and speaking, too much jargon is a bad idea. There is a balance that you can strike between the two sides, but this needs to be done carefully.

Over anything else, it is important to remember that you are speaking with other *people*. When you initiate conversations in a professional setting, you probably think more about making yourself look good than anything else. At the end of the day, you still interact with a human being. The people you speak with probably do not want to hear someone throwing out technical terms left and right, and they probably do not want to waste time figuring out what you are trying to say. Some key pieces of industry-specific jargon are great, but remember to use general, comprehensible words for most of your conversation.

Commercial Terminology

At first glance, the difference between professional and commercial vernacular might not seem that big. However, exchanging information professionally and discussing a specific product are very different functions. As such, you need to use different words for each situation.

To start, let us explore what the term "commercial" means in a broad context; As one HubSpot article puts it, *"Commercial use describes any activity in which you use a product or service for financial gain."* In conversations about commercial matters, you are selling, analyzing, or using a product. Commercial terminology, by extension, involves particular words used to talk about a product, idea, or brand. There is a lot of overlap with marketing terms in commercial conversations, so it is useful to know terms such as:

- **Channel:** The place where you introduce your product to potential consumers.
- **Keywords:** Words or phrases that potential consumers use to find your product.
- **Personalization:** Catering your product (and your marketing) to members of your consumer base.
- **Segmentation:** Dividing potential consumers into segments based on their characteristics, like demographics, location, or gender.

If this is the kind of conversation you plan on having frequently in the future, it is worth getting to know your way around the jargon of marketing and advertising. Those selling products should incorporate call-to-action words like now, fix, save, discover, and imagine and descriptive terms like simple, exclusive, deal, value, or opportunity.

The Right Words for Casual Social Conversations

Casual, friendly, or social conversations may seem like a no-brainer regarding vernacular—should not you just talk how you normally talk? Well, this can be a deceptively tricky arena to navigate.

If you know someone well, conversations and their accompanying vocabulary will flow naturally. However, talking with strangers is a different matter altogether. Depending on your cultural setting, geographical location, and demographic characteristics, casual conversation can look very different for different people. While you might feel awkward about it at first, it is a good idea to research casual vernacular if you are meeting strangers in a new place. Regional slang, idioms, or phrases can take you by surprise if you hear them for the first time while in a conversation, so preparing yourself is a smart first step. With this knowledge in mind, remember that respect, authenticity, and genuine curiosity are the bedrock of good interaction. In most cases, respect is the name of the game when it comes to strangers. While you do not have to be formal, it is best to use respectful and tactful phrases like:

- Would you happen to know ___?
- Pardon me/Excuse me...
- Would you mind ___?
- Would you be so kind as to ___?
- I would appreciate it if you could ___.

For instance, *"Would you mind telling me where the bathroom is?"* sounds much more polite than *"Where is the bathroom?"* and will often leave a better impression. Of course, throwing in a greeting like *"Hi,"* *"Hey,"* or *"Good morning"* is a safe bet, and please and thank-yous are a must if you want to be considered polite. While you do not necessarily have to speak like you are talking to your grandparents, starting respectfully and gradually becoming more casual as you advance in your conversations is always best.

Mirroring Speech Patterns and Tone

Have you ever been conversing with a close friend, only to notice that you are using the same speech patterns, phrases, and body language as them? Or maybe you still use a unique turn of phrase that you learned from an ex-boyfriend or girlfriend. This is perfectly natural and usually arises from an unconscious need to fit in. Friends, family, romantic relationships, and acquaintances can influence how we speak, move, and think. This phenomenon is called homophily, or the tendency toward similarity between people who spend time with each other. The more time you spend with someone, the more alike you will behave. Homophily is not just an abstract concept, either—according to one study of 6,000 students in grades 5 through 11, *"students choose a new friend among those who are similar to them [academically] 64%-81% more often than dissimilar ones."* Homophily is not just limited to one aspect of our lives, it can impact everything from work habits to substance use.

In the first few minutes of a conversation with a new person, the big picture of Homophily does not matter much. *After all, how can a person you have just met influence your behavior meaningfully?*

Before you write off the psychology of homophily, though, consider the mechanism through which homophily works: Mirroring. In the words of one Huffington Post article, *"Mirroring'—people that are your friends or people that like you in general, tend to physically mimic or mirror your behavior, vernacular, movements, etc.—is an example of the type of subconscious influence that your friends have over you."* Think back to that close friend or relative that has influenced the way you talk. Because you are so close and because you have spent so much time with that person, you begin to behave similarly. Knowing this, it is not a stretch to say that we generally behave similarly to people we like, right? By extension, you can subconsciously endear yourself to new people by mirroring their tone of voice, body language, and expressions.

In those first few seconds of a new conversation, mirroring can make a huge difference in how people perceive you. When you start conversations with new people, pay close attention to their posture and word choice, and try subtly mimicking it when it is your turn to speak. Mirroring can be done with the things we have already mentioned, like the tone of voice and expressions, but it can also be done with the content of the conversation itself. Repeating your partner's message in your own words is a great way to mirror that information and let them know that you are listening. Try to make your mirroring subtle enough that your partner does not notice. Being mimicked move-for-move or word-for-word can be unnerving, and it can also come across as mocking sometimes. Rather, keep an eye out for small movements and keywords that you can use throughout the conversation.

Just in case you are wondering, mirroring your conversational partner *does* work in most cases. In one 2011 study, one group of retail workers was instructed to mirror the behavior and speech of their customers, while another was instructed to try to sell products as they normally would. The group instructed to mirror their customers sold more products overall, and customers reported a more positive opinion of the store. Whether you are selling, networking, or just talking casually to a stranger, mirroring is bound to bring better results.

Authenticity and Uniqueness

From specific terminology to mirroring, there are a lot of different elements of socialization to keep track of. It can quickly get overwhelming for those not used to having many conversations with new people, leaving you feeling frazzled or on edge. While there are many different methods to make sure you leave a great first impression, all this cerebral processing can occasionally work against you—thinking too much about mirroring, word choice, or posture can give off an awkward vibe that your partner will pick up on.

As such, it is important to keep yourself grounded in reality; in essence, you are just exchanging information with a new person. Assuming that you are looking to build long-lasting relationships, maintaining authenticity and honesty with your conversational partner is extremely important. If you are nervous, there is no harm in acknowledging your feelings! Authenticity and honesty can have manifold positive effects regarding the quality of your interactions. First, let the other person know what is happening inside your head. If they feel the same as you, your honesty may put them at ease and make them more comfortable expressing themselves. Authenticity in the first few seconds of a conversation will also set the tone for the rest of your interaction, which will likely make interacting easier for both you and your partner.

How can you be more authentic in your conversations, then? According to one resource from Baylor Scott and White, *"authentic communication happens when we become more thoughtful with our words and our responses to others."* In short, being honest with your conversational partner starts with being honest with yourself. If you notice that you feel nervous or anxious, take a second and give yourself room to feel your emotions. Taking deep breaths, saying a couple of mental affirmations, and looking at the objective reality of a situation can all get you into a better mental space.

With all this information about first impressions, you might wonder how much first impressions matter in the long term. *If you only plan to speak to someone once, a good impression will not benefit you all that much, right?* Before you write off the long-term social, professional, and relational impact of first impressions, let us look at a particularly potent psychological phenomenon. The Halo Effect can impact your interactions beyond what you might imagine, and it centers completely around your first interaction with someone. In the next chapter, we will talk about the Halo Effect and how you can use it to your advantage.

CHAPTER 2

THE HALO EFFECT

S nap judgments, while common, are often completely wrong. To explore this, let us explore a common example: Imagine you are a hiring manager at a successful financial consulting firm. Like all other managers, you want your employees to be competent, responsible, committed, and to work hard. You are looking at the files of two new candidates you are interviewing, candidate A and candidate B.

Candidate A graduated high school with good grades, then took a gap year to work as a secretary in a small business. After some time, they returned to school, finishing their undergraduate work at a state school with a relatively high acceptance rate. They graduated with good grades and have been looking for a new job ever since.

Candidate B, on the other hand, attended an elite private school. Their grades are the same as Candidate A's, but they went to university after finishing high school. Candidate B also went to an exclusive Ivy League school and was involved in several clubs and events throughout their academic career. They finished college with good grades.

In this situation, which candidate do you think works harder? For many real-world hiring managers, the Ivy League graduate is considered to work harder, despite not having any work experience. In fact, the average career salaries of Ivy League graduates are a whopping 47% higher than those with degrees from non-Ivy League schools. As time goes on, this difference widens to a whopping 108%.

In reality, the difference between an Ivy League alumnus and a state school alumni involves many more factors than simply working hard—economic struggles, lack of resources, and demographic information can all affect which school someone attends. In this hypothetical situation, candidate A likely works just as hard as candidate B. The only difference between the two is an exclusive university name.

What Is the Halo Effect?

In the words of The Decision Lab, *"The halo effect is a cognitive bias that claims that positive impressions of people, brands, and products in one area positively influence our feelings in another area."* The term was first developed by American psychologist Edward Thorndike in the 1920s and was used to describe the attitudes of Army officers toward their soldiers. In Thorndike's original descriptions of the halo effect, superiors were likelier to describe their workers as either completely good or bad at tasks, leaving no room for nuance or elaboration. As much as it hurts our relationships with the people around us, the halo effect is ubiquitous among all demographics and cultures. In studying the halo effect, scientists have paid close attention to how looks and beauty standards affect how people perceive us.

For those trying to form new professional, commercial, or social relationships, this can easily sound like disheartening news. However, there are still a couple of things that you can do to turn this cognitive bias to your advantage.

How to Use the Halo Effect to Create a Good Impression

In the context of homophily and the halo effect, the dangers of a poor first impression may feel dire. However, the possibility that a good first impression can open may surprise you. In other words, you want to build yourself the perfect "halo" to present to new people.

Basics like dressing in the proper clothes for the situation, having clothes that fit well, keeping up with your hygiene, and maintaining open body language are all great starts. In professional and commercial situations, here are some things that will paint you as a stellar candidate:

- Getting to meetings or events early
- Researching the people, companies, or products that you are going to be interacting with
- A firm handshake
- Emphasizing your strengths and providing evidence
- Getting a friend or colleague to recommend you to people in their network.
- Show passion for your conversational message while you speak.
- Speak confidently, but ensure all parties get an opportunity to speak.

Circling back to our original description of the halo effect, we generally like associating with people like us. How you relate to people professionally or commercially does not necessarily need to be strictly professional—personability is just as important as competence, especially if you want to build long-term relationships with people in your field. Throughout your conversations, try to find commonalities between you and the person you speak with. *Are you from the same place? Did you go to the same schools? Do you share any similar interests or habits?* If you have trouble finding these connections between you and your partner, try looking for secondary and tertiary connections. Things like friendly rivalries between sports teams or schools may be a great way to connect with your audience, forming a link between your life experience and theirs. No matter what you come up with, always ensure that you remain professional, respectful, and curious in your interactions.

More casual conversations and social conversations are easier to navigate on this front. Finding connections between you and a stranger can be as simple as buying the same brand of coffee or going to the same corner store. Just like with professional and commercial halos, you can also bond with people over things like friendly rivalries between sports teams or general dislikes. In casual conversations, it can sometimes be difficult to know when you have stepped over the line. To avoid faux pas, never invalidate your partner's perspectives or opinions, and try your best to be friendly *and* respectful.

Sometimes, however, you will find that the halo you built is not working. These are the times in which you need to remember: You cannot win them all. When you cannot seem to find a connection, do not despair. Instead, think about what you might be able to do differently next time. If the conversation in question was a formal conversation like an interview, try reaching out to see what you could improve on.

The halo effect can be difficult to turn to your advantage when talking to someone for the first time. In groups, the mere idea of the halo effect may make you want to turn around and go home. However, the positive power of the halo effect can be drastically amplified when you use it properly in group settings. The next chapter will cover first impressions in groups and how to manage your professional, commercial, and social image.

CHAPTER 3

FIRST IMPRESSIONS IN GROUP SETTINGS

D epending on your disposition, the size of a group can either make or break the flow of your conversations. So far, we have only talked about one type of group conversation: the dyad or the two-person group. In dyads, the conversation should be about 50/50, with both parties asking questions, delivering responses, and exchanging information in equally share. In these situations, you will get a feel for your partner quickly, setting both of you at ease sooner. If one person leaves a two-person conversation, the conversation is over. As you will find, these attributes are very different from the attributes of conversations between bigger groups of people. This is partially why group conversations can be so intimidating. For introverts, making sure that everyone in a group understands your message can be mentally taxing, and fielding questions from multiple people can quickly become overwhelming. Additionally, the boundaries of groups and group conversations are not always as cut-and-dry as dyads. Similarly, leaving a group conversation can bring along another kind of anxiety.

However, our work and social lives often require us to interact with people in groups. Group socialization is simply a part of life, whether it is team meetings at work or parties with friends and acquaintances. To set your mind at ease, it may help to understand how group socialization works at a basic level.

The Basics of Group Size and Leadership

So, we know what a dyad is. There are also triads (or three-person groups), which may still be within your comfort zone. However, bigger groups with four or more people can start to feel busy and overwhelming. This could be explained by the number of relationships within the group—a dyad only has one relationship (between you and your partner). A triad has two relationships. A big seven-member discussion, however, has 21 relationships. Aside from being a lot to keep track of, it also means that you are in relation with six other people. By extension, you will likely feel pressure to amuse, inform, rebuke, or confirm everyone in the group, making your job as a group member much harder. Entering and leaving the group can also be difficult, as large groups may not specifically acknowledge when you join or leave.

Within groups, whether professional, commercial, or social, there tends to be striation of some kind. While it may not always be clear, there is usually an impromptu group leader. In sociology, there are two kinds of group leaders:

1. **Instrumental leaders.** This kind of leader is goal-oriented and will prioritize whatever the group's goal is. Instrumental leaders pursue the group's goal even if it causes conflict or alienation among members.
2. **Expressive leaders.** Expressive leaders are relationship-oriented, and they tend to prioritize harmony and equal engagement from all group members.

As you might have guessed, instrumental leaders are more common in professional settings—discussion leaders in a classroom, team leads in a work meeting, and club presidents in an organization are all examples of this kind of leader. Expressive leaders, on the other hand, are more suited to casual and social settings, like a host at a dinner party. While instrumental leaders tend to be professional and expressive leaders tend to be social, both types of leadership can occur in all kinds of groups. In bigger groups, there may also be both types of leadership displayed by different group members.

For you, as a new member of a group conversation, this is an important distinction. If you enter a work meeting expecting an expressive leadership style, you might be a little taken aback when encountering an instrumental leader. Conversely, anticipating an instrumental leadership style in an expressive environment can paint you a little standoffish or awkward. Before you enter larger group conversations, think about the context, setting, and people involved to determine what kind of leadership style you will encounter.

Aside from leadership roles, group members can fall into different roles based on the context and size of the group. In general, these roles tend to be clear because of context clues. For instance, roles in the workplace are usually very well-defined because of the setting, while casual socialization among peers puts you in the same role as everyone else.

No matter your role, be aware of your thoughts, opinions, and knowledge. Think back to mirroring and homophily (mimicking the people around you to endear yourself to your audience). The same concepts exist in group settings, sometimes even more so because of the number of relationships you have with others in a group. While mirroring conversational messages, tone, and body language can be a great way to align yourself with people, it can also lead to groupthink. Groupthink, or when people agree with the perceived desires of a group to fit in, can result in poor outcomes in all situations. Groupthink is especially problematic in groups with instrumental leadership, as pressure from the top can result in uninformed or short-sighted decision-making. In social situations, groupthink can lead to alienation and weakened social relationships.

As it happens, you already know the antidote for this potential issue—authenticity. Being honest with yourself and your conversational partners is a great way to avoid the dangers of groupthink *and* endear yourself to a group. Asking clarifying questions is another great way to engage in a group conversation, and it can also take some of the pressure of speaking off you. As long as you speak confide/ntly and respectfully, you can communicate successfully with a new group just as you would with one-on-one conversations.

Introducing Yourself to a Group

No matter what kind of group you find yourself in, it is important to introduce yourself to everyone. However, you may notice that the point at which you first join the group and the point at which you introduce yourself are different in many cases. This is perfectly normal, and you should not feel pressure to introduce yourself immediately after you enter a group setting.

The introduction you make will largely depend on the context of your situation. Introductions can be easily divided by the type of interaction you are looking to initiate:

1. **Professional.** There are numerous instances in which you will be expected to introduce yourself professionally, from group interviews to team meetings and beyond. At the core of your introduction, there are three things that you need to convey; Who you are, what you do, and anything else your audience needs to know. Chances are that the first two things you convey (who you are and what you do) will not change from conversation to conversation. For instance, a basic professional introduction might look something like this:

    Hello! My name is ___, and I am a software engineer at ___ company.

Depending on the situation, you may want to get more specific with your job title or role in a company. For example, your full job title might be better suited to your first time at a company team meeting. Additionally, terms that indicate your organizational level *(junior, associate, senior)* may be useful to emphasize your role. From here, give a few brief sentences informing your audience of other important facts about you. Things such as your career goals or aspirations in the next five years, accomplishments, and your reason for being in the group are all great options. Sometimes, you will hear professional introductions *(especially for jobseekers and junior-level employees)* called elevator pitches.

In more formal settings, it is best to stick to solely professional facts. However, introducing yourself to new coworkers can sometimes be a little more laid-back. If this sounds like something you might encounter, your elevator pitch might include some basic personal information, like one or two fun hobbies, how many pets you have, or where you are from. Incorporating these elements into your professional introduction can make you seem less stiff and more personable, encouraging other professionals to interact with you more. At the end of your introduction, leaving your door open is always a great idea. If you encourage people to approach you in the future, they probably will! Phrases like *"Feel free to reach out to me if you have any questions!"* or *"I am looking forward to working with everyone!"* are great send-offs that will leave your audience feeling good about future interactions. Avoid controversial, disrespectful, or otherwise unsavory topics in your elevator pitch.

2. **Commercial.** Oddly, your commercial introduction will look a lot like your professional introduction. In general,

you will want to include the same three things in this introduction *(who you are, what you do, and other relevant information)*. However, marketing vernacular or branding terms will play much more in your commercial introduction. First, define your product exactly—this can be a personal brand, a service you perform, or an actual physical or virtual product you sell. Rather than conveying information solely about yourself in this case, you will want to integrate more information about your expertise and the utility of your product into your elevator pitch. Before you go into group situations, try writing down key points about your product and your expertise that you can highlight in your introduction.

With a couple of basic ideas sketched, you will want to figure out how to cater your elevator pitch to your audience. *How will using your product affect their business or company? What pressure points or struggles can your product alleviate? What distinguishes your product from other similar products?* Before you head into conversations, consider doing in-depth research about your audience to make your elevator pitch airtight. Aside from this, you generally do not want your introduction to be too formal or buttoned-up, as this might convey a sense of nervousness. Additionally, you do not want your initial introduction to be too long or wordy—no one wants to sit through an advertisement for longer than they must! Instead, it will help your case to be personable, authentic, and brief.

3. **Social/casual.** As group introductions go, social introductions are perhaps some of the most worrisome for introverts. Being too formal can be perceived as nervousness or awkwardness, and being too casual can be perceived as disrespectful or flippant. That being said, it

is not a bad idea to simply adapt the core of your professional introduction to a social situation. That is, include things about who you are, what you do, and other relevant information (in broader, more casual terms). The outline of your casual introduction might look something like:

> Hi everyone! I am Kate's friend, ___. I am from New York and so excited to be here celebrating New Year's with you all!

Some other facts to include might be what you are doing at the function, what you do in your free time, and what activities you are good at. More so than other types of introductions, causal introductions are very relational. If you can find a way to tie yourself to other group members (*I met Kate back in college, Steven and I work together, and Peter and I used to be neighbors*), you will be in a great position to leverage that person's social connections. Finally, those attending events like housewarmings or dinner parties cannot go wrong with thanking the host at the end of the introduction.

In all contexts, it is usually best to keep your initial introduction short and sweet. A couple of sentences of basic information can be more than enough to boost your audience's sense of connection with you. If your audience starts asking more questions about you or your background after your elevator pitch or introduction, feel free to start elaborating further.

First Impressions in a Group Setting

First impressions in a group can be difficult to manage, given that every member may have their own opinions or cognitive biases. However, the core of first impressions in group settings is essentially the same as one-on-one conversations. Good hygiene, genuine curiosity, authenticity, open body language, and happy or neutral expressions are good places to start. While still a great option for endearing yourself to a group, Mirroring can suddenly get very confusing—whom are you mirroring? What if people in the group have different body language, speech patterns, or expressions from one another?

More so than one-on-one conversations, group settings require you to read the room properly. This is not negotiable, especially considering you might not know everyone in the group. The basics of reading a room are:

- **Simply observing.** At this point, you already know that body language is important to look at. However, did you know that 55% of communication is entirely nonverbal? Out of our total methods for communication, over half is determined by body language, 38% is vocal, and only 7% is determined by the actual words we say. Knowing this, even the smallest expressions or body language changes can suddenly mean a lot. The space between people, who are sitting near, and whether people are standing or sitting can tell you a lot about the group's mood.

- **Controlling how much you speak (and ensuring that everyone else speaks just as much as you).** By necessity, watching out for nonverbal cues means keeping your input and comments to a minimum. Of course, answer and ask questions if speaking with someone directly. However, try to listen and look more than you speak. If you can, try to piece together existing relationships in the group, and figure out if any existing relationships seem important *(if any group members are friends, colleagues, siblings, etc.).* To see how people interact with each other, open-ended questions are preferable.

- **Accurately interpreting your observations.** Empathy is a great tool in big groups to keep in your back pocket. Try to understand what is going on in people's lives and why they say what they say. If something does not make sense, or if you do not completely understand something that has been said, do not be afraid to admit your confusion. To this end, asking clarifying questions is a good move.

Now that we have reviewed some basic to-dos on your group socialization checklist, let us discuss some not-to-dos. In groups, you may feel pressured to insert yourself into conversations and engage immediately. In reality, this might hurt you if you do not pick the right moment to jump in. Instead, try waiting for a good opening where you can introduce yourself. When multiple conversations occur within a group, try not to get distracted from the interaction you are having—getting distracted during a conversation is rude and ultimately shows your partners that you do not care about the topic of conversation. In other words, ensure your phone stays in your pocket for the whole conversation. Finally, try to keep your emotions at bay. Sharing your opinions to engage in a conversation is one thing, but getting emotional can lead to poor social and professional outcomes. If you feel overwhelmed, frustrated, or very emotional, try excusing yourself from the group and taking time to recover.

While group conversations can be nerve-wracking, they can also offer several benefits for introverts. Interacting with several people in a group can take some of the pressure of speaking off you and expose you to more interesting perspectives. Overall, you will find that group conversations are easy to engage in as long as you keep a cool head and are respectful.

At this point in your conversational journey, you have likely initiated and participated in several conversations. Whether with strangers in a coffee shop or coworkers at your new job, striking up a good conversation is usually easier than you think. The purpose of conversations, however, is not to have one conversation. Rather, you are probably looking to build long-term, meaningful connections with people. These connections only happen with repeated interactions, meaning your job is not done. In the next book, we will dive into the world of rapport and how you can build rapport with strangers in no time.

Book 3: Lasting Connections Through Rapport

Building Bridges - The Art of Cultivating
Enduring Relationships with Effective Rapport

Kirsten Rae Evans

TABLE OF CONTENTS

INTRODUCTION

Consider, for a moment, your close connections in your personal network. These connections can be friends, relatives, or even spouses. Across all your closest relationships, *what do you notice?* Maybe you have running jokes with your friends, or maybe you and your spouse experienced a funny event together. At the very least, your family members or guardians have known you since you were an adult, which comes with a lot of closeness ingrained. At the core of these connections is one huge thing—time. The amount of time you spend with people is a sign of your closeness to them and a reason for that closeness in the first place. With time comes trust, and with trust comes a sturdy and long-lasting relationship.

Introverts looking to make impactful and meaningful connections with new people may succeed in having conversations. Still, many get stuck when advancing a relationship to the next level. Many people prefer to let this process happen gradually and naturally, but this can lead to a connection drought. To move a relationship from one level to another, you need to initiate a mechanism inviting trust and time.

CHAPTER 1

BASICS OF RAPPORT

Picture this—you have started several successful conversations with strangers at a local coffee shop and are feeling good about your conversational skills. Now, you are looking to take your interactions to the next step. In other words, you want to make your new acquaintances into friends or professional connections. The only problem is that you do not know how to make that happen.

Many people wind up in this phase, confident enough to converse once or twice but not confident enough to do anything else. Recent high school and university graduates often find themselves in this dilemma, typically because the connections they might have had in school were developed by proximity. In adulthood, where you do not have to attend semester-long classes or eat lunch in the cafeteria, the opportunities for friendships via proximity change dramatically. Forming meaningful connections can feel impossible in a world where you do not have to be friends with the people you see every day.

For many, this may feel like a dead end. Meaningful connections with people are not for the faint of heart. The only way to continue developing and cultivating a relationship with someone is through continued interactions. In short—rinse and repeat. Over time, having regular, intentional, and impactful conversations with someone will build rapport.

What Is Rapport?

MasterClass states, *"Rapport is a harmonious relationship between people who have established mutual trust. Building rapport is how humans connect, identify shared feelings, and establish two-way communication."* For our purposes, we will also define rapport as mutual trust intending to engage again in the future. In other words, your goal in speaking with people is to form meaningful professional and social relationships. This kind of rapport does not happen just out of the blue. You may speak with your local barista every day, but that does not mean you will form a meaningful relationship with them. Rather, meaningful rapport is built after repetitive interactions beyond typical, everyday small talk.

Often, simply talking and interacting with people is not enough. Viewing rapport as an equal trade between you and someone else can be an unsettling prospect, especially if the relationship is more professional than social. For some, a more useful perspective may be that of a caretaker or keeper—in other words, building a good rapport with people is an act of kindness or service. Through this paradigm, you can start to see yourself as a valuable contributor to the quality of other people's lives. Conversely, if you start thinking of yourself as providing something of value to others, you will probably be more inclined to put yourself out there more regularly.

The Benefits of Creating Rapport

To show the power that rapport has over social, mental, and cognitive abilities, let us look at a university classroom. In one study from Auburn University, researchers looked at the effects of rapport among students' mental health, interest in the subject matter, and academic performance in an introductory psychology class. Those who had developed a rapport with professors consistently showed better mental and emotional health, higher interest in the coursework, and better grades than their peers who had not developed a rapport with professors.

In social contexts, it is plain to see why rapport is important for long-term friendships. However, building trust with people around you at work, school, and other professional spheres is just as important. Think back to the last bad team project you experienced professionally or academically—*how would the experience have been different if you already had a good rapport with your group?* Everyone wants to be around people that they trust and respect, and your professional life greatly benefits from putting effort into building rapport with your peers. At work, building a good rapport with your coworkers can result in the following:

- Making everyone feel more involved in the culture and mission of your workplace
- Good group dynamics in future teams
- Effective and efficient communication between employees
- Improve team performance overall

Again, it can sometimes be helpful to think of this trust-building as a service you offer to the people around you, understanding their needs and making their lives easier. An enjoyable, respectful, supportive workplace does not have to start at the top, and you can easily make people like you by building strong professional relationships. If you are in a managerial or senior position at work, rapport is doubly important for the people you manage. According to one Gallup poll, employees who strongly agreed with the statement *"I feel I can talk with my manager about nonwork-related issues"* reported having 47% more engagement at work than those who disagreed. Similarly, people who agreed that *"I feel I can approach my manager with any type of question"* were 53% more engaged than their counterparts who disagreed with the statement. In short, rapport is key for boosting engagement, productivity, and worker well-being for everyone in the workplace.

Commercial settings are no different. Building rapport with clients, customers, and other businesses in your field can boost your business's productivity and widen your consumer base. Despite the plethora of channels businesses and brands use to reach potential customers, word-of-mouth marketing (sometimes called WOMM) is still one of the most effective marketing methods. In one source from Nielsen, 92% of consumers believe recommendations from friends and family over all forms of advertising. When you use a WOMM strategy in commercial situations, you are essentially leveraging your consumers' connections with other people. By building rapport with one audience, you can effectively double the reach of your product when consumers spread knowledge of your business to people in their network.

The Golden Rule of Rapport

At this point, you have probably gathered the basics of how to build rapport. You can inevitably build rapport with others through things like:

- Emphasizing commonalities
- Actively listening to your partner(s)
- Remembering crucial information
- Asking questions
- Mirroring

There is another major factor in rapport. However, that is crucial to your future relationships. Authenticity is a buzzword nowadays, but that does not mean you should ignore it. Being honest with yourself and your conversational partner(s) is a huge aspect of getting to know people and building rapport. After all, mutual trust requires some trust that other people will accept you for who you are, does not it?

As a result, being your authentic self is the golden rule of building rapport. Humans are strangely good at knowing when people are fake or dishonest, so inauthenticity often garners poor or undesirable results. The science behind detecting authenticity is wild—one 2014 study determined that infants as young as 19 months old were able to detect dishonesty and emotional inauthenticity through three main cues:

1. Contextual congruence of the emotion shown *(how well—or poorly—a particular emotion fits a particular situation)*.
2. How much the emotion was exaggerated.
3. How the emotion was communicated.

Not only were these infants able to detect inauthentic emotion, but they could also detect it consistently. Basically, humans are hardwired to see when other humans are being dishonest. If a 19-month-old infant can see when you are bored with a conversation, your coworkers, acquaintances, and friends will also be able to see it.

Authenticity starts with being honest with yourself, which can be tricky. Consciously acknowledging what you feel and why you might be feeling it takes practice, and the only way to practice is through having more conversations. Whenever you are talking with new people, make sure to periodically check in with yourself—how are you feeling? Are you listening to what your partner is saying? Is there anything that is bothering you or distracting you? In that same vein, remember to trust your intuition while interacting with people. One great way to convey authenticity is by asking your partner questions, specific questions to which you want to know the answers. If anything in your partner's response strikes you as interesting, follow it up!

Remembering names and being yourself is a great start to building rapport, but you can always do more to show people you care. Next, we will dive into the nitty-gritty details of what you can think, say, and do that will boost your rapport with the people in your life.

CHAPTER 2

THE DETAILS OF BUILDING STRONG RAPPORT

ommunicating with people intending to build rapport can be a challenge, even when you know all the right things to do. On a practical level, speaking with people about personal information can sometimes feel invasive or aggressive, which usually results in bad outcomes for everyone involved. Putting potential friends, customers, and business partners on the defensive is ultimately not what you want.

How do you build personal trust, then? Discretion, properly-worded questions and answers, and equal exchange of information is the key to being personable without intrusive.

Get Personal

One of the scariest things about talking with strangers is that they are strangers. You cannot always see the potential pitfalls or faux pas that might pop up when you have an authentic, meaningful conversation. Whether it is a bad experience at a company or a personal fallout with someone, you really do not know your conversational partner well enough to talk about super personal information. Staying away from the typical no-nos like religion and politics is a good start, but it often is not enough. Some other topics to stay away from include:

- Health
- Personal finances
- Gossip
- Deeply personal relationships *(family, romantic relationships, close friends, etc.)*
- Substances *(like drugs or alcohol)*
- Conflicts, both personal and professional

Similarly, questions regarding race, ethnicity, gender, and sexual orientation need to be navigated carefully. While most people will happily discuss their identity, respect should always be your top priority. Questions like *"Where are you from?"* can sometimes be offensive, especially if asked randomly. Asking questions about sensitive topics like one's identity can make people feel like they do not belong, or worse, you are using it to determine your opinions of them. Of course, you *(hopefully)* do not mean to go around offending people by asking personal questions. If you want to broach the topic of someone's background but do not want to come across as invasive, try talking a bit about your background first. Sometimes, doing this will prompt your conversational partner to start discussing their background, negating the need for an awkward question. If you need to ask questions, choose your words carefully, and listen to any feedback your partner gives you. In many cases, it is better to simply avoid the topic of self-identity altogether in professional and commercial settings.

Now that you know more about potentially sensitive topics to avoid, let us dive deeper into what behavior you should focus on as you build rapport.

What Was Your Name Again?

Hopefully, you know by now that remembering someone's name is one of the most basic things you can do to build rapport with someone. If you are anything like me, remembering names can sometimes be a real struggle. One minute, someone is introducing themselves, and I am feeling good about striking up a conversation, and just a few minutes later, I am racking my brain to recall their name. There are several possible reasons why this might happen—an already-full mental capacity, stress, and generally bad memory are all culprits. Going into conversations, the fear of forgetting names can prevent you from focusing on the quality of the interaction entirely!

Luckily, there are a few things you can do to try and improve your short-term memory. First off, staying in the moment and actively listening to your partner is crucial to remembering their name. These two things often happen naturally when you are genuinely curious about your partner. As they introduce themselves, take a good look at their face and try to associate it with their name.

There is another great trick to try if you find yourself forgetful. After someone's told you their name, use it! Say their name immediately after they have introduced themselves, both to make sure that you heard them right as well as to cement it into your memory. If they have a name that is hard to pronounce, make sure that you are saying it right before using it in other contexts. A simple *"Sorry, how do you say your name?"* can go a long way in showing that you care about the conversation you are having. Throughout the conversation, use their name after questions. Before you leave, use a phrase like *"It was great to meet you, ____! Hope we talk again soon!"* or something similar. While you do not want to overdo it and run the risk of sounding strange, saying a person's name in conversation can improve their engagement in the interaction. According to one Michigan State University article, using a person's name regularly *"creates a culture of respect, recognition, and consideration for the discussion."*

Sometimes, despite our honest intentions and our best efforts, a name will escape us. In these cases, try your best to remember what your partner's name is. Think back to when they first introduced themselves—What were they doing as they were speaking? Can you remember the letter that their name starts with? Does the name sound like another word? Anything you can think of to jog your memory is helpful. If you really, really cannot remember, you may just have to swallow your pride and ask them. A quick question like *"I am so sorry, but what is your name again?"* is still polite, while a little annoying for you. Alternatively, asking for the spelling of a name or the proper pronunciation of a name can also let you hear the person's name again.

Ask for Help or Advice

Even amongst close friends, asking for and receiving help can be a difficult hurdle. A lot of times, we do not want to burden people or annoy them by asking for assistance. In reality, most people are more than willing to lend a helping hand, even if it is for something as simple as directions. Aside from making your life easier in a small way, asking your conversational partner for help allows them to perform a service for you. Helping someone else out usually makes people feel good, and it can show them that they have agency and importance in your interactions.

As with most things when it comes to talking with people, you cannot always win them all. Asking for help at the right times is crucial, and only ask if you see that your partner is engaged in the conversation, listening to you actively, and showing positive emotional and verbal cues. If you are not feeling secure in how the conversation is going or are having trouble gauging your partner's attitude toward the interaction, asking for help with something can give you some insight. When your partner agrees to help enthusiastically, immediately, or with an openly positive attitude, they are probably enjoying the conversation. If your partner hesitates, looks uncomfortable, or flat-out refuses, it may be time to end the conversation.

Some good things to ask for may include:

- Directions to somewhere close

- What time, day, or day of the month is it
- To borrow a phone charger
- Advice on things to purchase
- Advice on how to do a hobby or fun activity properly

And anything else that is both small and applicable to your situation.

Know Your Customer's Personality Type

If you have been in the business world for a while, you have probably seen a lot of information circulating about the Myers-Briggs personality assessment. For those who do not know, the test separates people into groups based on their attitudes toward four different personality aspects; introversion versus extroversion, sensing versus intuition, thinking versus feeling and judging versus perceiving. After the assessment, participants get a set of letters like INTJ or ESFP that supposedly shows what kind of person they are. Using information about someone's Myers-Briggs may or may not work for social interactions. After all, you want to look at your friends as real, complex people with lives rather than simply a collection of traits. For professionals and entrepreneurs, on the other hand, Myers-Briggs and other personality tests like it can perform a vital function.

In the case of Myers-Briggs, the letters indicate four pieces of information about a person:

1. Where your attention lies most of the time.
2. How you take in and process information.
3. How you make decisions.
4. How you deal with the world.

Different personality tests will assess different traits in people, but they will all ultimately give you bite-sized pieces of information you can use in your interactions. For those in the professional and commercial spheres, personality test-like information can give you an easily-digestible and easily-understandable way to categorize people. When considering the consumer base of a small business, for instance, it might be difficult to describe the type of customer that requests services. Without a framework for defining how people behave and think, coming up with terms on your own gets hard. Categorized like the ones we have already mentioned, however, can allow you to effectively deal with customers to achieve your professional goals. In commercial settings, understanding potential consumers will allow you to do market segmentation or divide your consumers based on their demographic, regional, or personal information. Breaking the markets into small, manageable pieces allows you to cater your approach to each segment, resulting in better outcomes.

Why does this matter in conversations? Well, personality can also help you navigate one-on-one and group interactions as well. Hypothetically, imagine that you are the owner of a small virtual business. In front of you are two rooms—one room holds a direct, brisk, and relatively quiet customer, and the other room holds a customer that is indirect, upbeat, and laid-back. If your goal is to sell your product and generate business, how does your approach change between the two rooms? Imagine if you were able to have access to this information before walking into every business meeting. Chances are, you had to be more well-equipped to navigate professional and commercial conversations with customers. Information about one's personality and traits is also great to have within a company, especially for managers or senior-level employees. Knowing at a glance how people interact with the world and how people process information is a great tool for business people, whether you are a solo entrepreneur or a junior employee at a big company.

Before your next big professional or commercial conversation, incorporate personality type into your research. Platforms like

LinkedIn are great for seeing what other professionals have to say about your conversational partner, and they will also give you some insight into your partner's professional presence. If you have professional connections that you are close with, ask them for useful information and leverage your relationship. Sentences like "I have a big meeting coming up with the executives of XYZ company. Do you have any insight into their attitudes or personalities?" may be a good way to reach out and research.

Feedback

Sometimes, we cannot provide feedback on people's performance or abilities. Giving someone feedback in a social setting can be quite offensive, as the other person may think that you are judging them. Giving someone feedback in the workspace is similarly fraught and can easily become unfavorable if conveyed in the wrong tone. However, in the right contexts, feedback can be an awesome way of building rapport with people.

First off, let us make a key distinction—giving feedback and giving critiques are two very different things. The critique focuses solely on three factors:

1. Identifying and explaining poor or undesirable outcomes.
2. Things that have happened in the past.
3. Identifying weaknesses in someone's approach.

When you critique someone, you are not just looking at how they handle problems. Rather, you are effectively looking for how they handle problems *incorrectly*. If you have ever seen films like Jon Favreau's *Chef* or Disney's *Ratatouille*, you will recognize this trait about food critics. Critique as both an activity and a profession is to point out everything you have done wrong in a given situation. When you are having a conversation with a new person, pointing out all their flaws and shortcomings is a surefire way to make yourself seem rude and unprofessional.

Feedback, on the other hand, is not nearly as ruthless as critique. Instead of focusing on all the negative aspects of a situation, feedback is centered around:

1. Identifying and explaining goals for a situation.
2. Things that could happen in the future.
3. Identifying strengths in someone's approach and supporting them so they can do well in the future.

Almost immediately, there is a noticeable shift to a feedback-based approach. Rather than brutally pointing out people's mistakes, feedback explores someone's strengths and areas in which they can improve. Feedback essentially validates the things that someone does well while simultaneously suggesting things that they could do to improve. In the workplace, this is an invaluable skill to learn. Making people feel supported, appreciated, and important is a great way to build rapport over time, and it can also make people feel more comfortable asking questions.

Feedback is much preferable to critique, but you should still be careful about where and when you offer feedback to people. In almost all instances, you should wait until someone explicitly asks for feedback before jumping in. Additionally, you generally will not be giving feedback to people at a higher level than you (seniors, company executives, and other professionals you do not know well). On the flip side, people may ask for your feedback if you have expertise in a particular area or sometimes if they want to get an objective opinion on a situation. In all regards, your feedback should always be respectful, kind, and constructive.

The specifics of rapport are easy to learn but can sometimes be difficult to implement in everyday interactions. Now that you are equipped with all the knowledge you need, though, you can start introducing rapport-building tools into your daily conversations. Before you know it, you will have developed new personal and professional connections in no time! The next topic we'll look into are some ways in which you can build rapport outside those everyday conversations, so you can take your relationships to the next level.

CHAPTER 3

BUILDING RAPPORT

Conversational rapport is one thing—maybe you have built up some trust with a colleague at work, or maybe you have interesting conversations with the same person at your coffee shop every day. This is an amazing accomplishment! You have contributed to your social and professional networks, and now you feel relatively confident when speaking to these people.

For professional and commercial relationships, this is usually where the rapport-building stops. Hanging out with colleagues after work or taking a client out to lunch are certainly trust-based activities, but you probably would not consider these people to be your friends. In the case of introverted people, this is typically where things get very hard in a social context. Bringing people from casual acquaintances into your inner social circle is a daunting task, especially if you do not feel confident in your abilities to make the transition successfully.

To explain this, we will turn back to the principles of psychology. Renowned social psychologist Robin Dunbar is responsible for the development of Dunbar's number, or the number of stable relationships that you can maintain at any time. This concept has been around since its inception in the 1990s, and the theory claims that one person can only have about 150 meaningful connections at once. More recently, however, Dunbar has continued his research into social and personal relationships, developing an entirely new theory. While the number 150 is still average for meaningful relationships, Dunbar now postulates that there are many separate friendship circles that we use to categorize our network.

Depending on where you are in your journey of becoming a conversationalist, you might want to prioritize one friendship circle over another. For instance, people who want to develop closer friendships will look primarily at the innermost circle of their network. After you have determined an area of focus, it is time to implement some rapport-building techniques to achieve your goals.

Rapport Beyond a Conversation

Conversations are a great way to bond, but they are not necessarily the only way. If you are stuck in the same place, talking about the same things, with the same person for a prolonged period, you might find that you eventually run out of steam. Knowing how to keep an interaction going is a good skill, but it should not be the only thing you rely on.

When we talk about those circle 5 or circle 15 connections, we are usually talking about people that you do things with. Hobbies or nonwork activities that you have in common are the ideal way to spend time with friends and social acquaintances. Professional and commercial connections benefit greatly from activities as well, and bonding activities can result in long-term, successful connections for all parties. In short, you need to learn how to make plans with people.

In all situations and contexts, here are some things you can do to form closer relationships with people:

- **Create common goals or missions.** In workplaces or in academic settings, this can sometimes happen naturally—you are in the same team working on a project, and you suddenly find that you have become a lot closer with the people around you. Alternatively, the same kind of thing happens with volunteering or altruistic endeavors. This bonding does not just happen because you are in the same place, either. In one study out of Hong Kong, researchers examined the relationship between shared company goals and the exchange of information between 190 different managers. In other words, how likely were people to have a conversation with others if they knew they shared the same mission? The study concluded that a shared goal drastically increased the likelihood that two people would converse with each other. Shared goals do not have to be limited to the workplace, though. A shared goal between you and a social acquaintance can be something as small as deciding on the best coffee shop in town or figuring out the directions to a particular shop. Another term you might recognize for this is problem-solving. In essence, discussing problems and working together to find a solution will bring you and your conversational partners closer, even if the problem in question is a small one.

- **Do something adventurous or fun.** Often, this option is reserved for people that you already have a great conversational rapport. Clients or coworkers that you have known for years, acquaintances that you see all the time, and neighbors that you know well are good candidates for this sort of thing. Meanwhile, going skydiving with a new client is a surefire way to never get their business again! That being said, the activity you choose does not necessarily need to be as bold as skydiving. Depending on the person you are with, something as simple as trying out new cuisines may work just fine. Adventure does not have to be extremely active, either. Entertainment you do not normally consume, like comedy shows, play productions, or theme parks, presents a great option to take a break from conversations *(while still having fun and bonding)*. If you choose to do something adventurous, make sure to match the activity to the person. If someone is afraid of heights, for example, maybe opt for a trip to the aquarium rather than a roller coaster.

- **Have a meal together.** In many cultures, shared meals and shared cooking is a societal norms. In the global West, this, unfortunately, is not the case for many people. One British survey led by our old friend Robin Dunbar found that the average adult eats at least half of their weekly meals alone, even though 76% of respondents claimed that communal eating is a good form of relationship building. Additionally, nearly 70% of respondents in the study said that they had never shared a meal with any of their neighbors. While there are many potential reasons why people do not eat together, shared meals are an excellent way of displaying mutual trust. As always, you should cater your approach to your conversational partner—a coffee and a quick bite to eat is best suited for a work colleague, while a full-length lunch or brunch is better for social friends.

Cashing In on Your Hook

If you recall the core parts of a conversation, you may remember the original hook that you set out to use in your interactions. This is essentially the reason why you are having a conversation in the first place or the general theme of the conversations you have with a particular person.

While your hook might have changed throughout the process of speaking to people, it is still a good idea to have a conversational hook in your back pocket. You do not have to write down all your hook ideas, but general concepts like:

I just moved here, and I want to make at least one close friend in this area.

Or;

I just got hired at this company, and I want to have at least two work friends that I can talk to about work problems.

Are a good place to start. In the context of developing long-term rapport with people, your goal should be to get as close to your hook as possible. Acknowledging your hook in conversation may help with this. Let us look at one example to get a sense of how this might help you. In this situation, Person 1 has just moved to a new place. Their hook is, *"I just moved here, and I want to make at least one close friend in this area."* Acknowledging this in a conversation with an acquaintance might look like this:

PERSON 1: THANKS SO MUCH FOR TRYING OUT THAT NEW COFFEE SHOP WITH ME. I HAD A GREAT TIME!

PERSON 2: I HAD AN AWESOME TIME TOO! WE SHOULD DO IT AGAIN SOON.

PERSON 1: I AM GLAD TO HEAR YOU SAY THAT. SINCE I AM NEW TO THIS AREA AND I DO NOT KNOW ANYONE HERE, IT IS NICE TO HAVE SOMEONE TO WALK AROUND WITH. WANT TO MEET UP AGAIN NEXT WEEK?

PERSON 2: SOUNDS GREAT!

In this case, Person 1 brought up their conversational hook in an authentic way. On an emotional level, saying aloud that you (a) enjoyed spending time with someone and (b) do not have any friends nearby is a very vulnerable and authentic sentiment. Often, this sense of vulnerability, honesty, and authenticity paints you as a genial, open person. Additionally, notice the emphasis that both parties put on future events. Talking a little bit about the future is a great way to express interest in becoming closer friends with someone, and even something as simple as using the future tense can work in your favor.

Building one-on-one rapport, like having one-on-one conversations, is an easy skill to acquire with enough practice and confidence. Of course, there are several instances in which you might want to build meaningful rapport with entire groups of people. In the next book, you will learn how to apply the rules of rapport to groups of people in multiple contexts.

Book 4: Building Meaningful Connections

From Interaction to Impact -Crafting Deep
Relationships in a Shallow World

Kirsten Rae Evans

TABLE OF CONTENTS

INTRODUCTION

Imagine that you are a job seeker walking into a local job fair. You sign in, grab a bite to eat and a beverage, and… Then you are at a loss. There are so many vendors and people walking around that the entire scene quickly becomes overwhelming. For some, the first instinct in this type of situation would be to simply leave. Others might try to initiate conversations with people, only to find themselves feeling stuck and awkward.

In situations like this, it is easy to imagine that you are the only one who is feeling out of place. However, you are rarely alone in this feeling. Learning about professional conversations in adulthood can be tough, especially given that most of us do not have exposure to these kinds of interactions until we are already in the workforce. As a result, we often feel like we are failing in our networking efforts, even if it is not true. However, it is never too late to learn how to network effectively. Just like any other acquired skill, a bit of networking practice can go a long way in preparing you for a world of new professional connections.

CHAPTER 1

GROUP STRUCTURE THEORY

C hances are, you have had a poor team-based experience before, either at work or at school. Being in this position is one of the worst feelings, namely because being placed in a bad group can spell trouble for your academic and career goals. From team members who do not carry their weight to toxic leadership dynamics, no one wants to get caught up in the drama of a bad team. Group settings are inevitable, unfortunately, and you can find yourself in the middle of a group in nearly all contexts in your life. House parties, work meetings, and academic groups can all potentially turn into poor group experiences. When you are a stranger to the group, the opportunity for things to turn sour might seem to grow before your eyes.

From this perspective, being in a group may seem like one of the least favorable methods of interacting with people. *With so many things that can go wrong, why would you ever choose to participate in a group conversation?*

Before you write off participating in a group, think about all the benefits that group communication can offer your social and professional life. When you speak successfully to a group, you are also effectively leveraging the personal network of everyone in the group. This widens your chance for professional opportunities, networking, and meeting new people in a social context. A group may also have more collective knowledge and wisdom than a single contact, and most people are more than happy to share information with you. Group conversations also offer a benefit that may appeal strongly to introverts—that is, the pressure of the conversation is shared. You do not have to speak for the entire time, and there may even be times when you can simply sit back and listen.

Knowing more about a group's structure and makeup can make these situations far less anxiety-inducing. At this point, you likely know that all groups have a leader, either designated or impromptu. Still, there are several other aspects of group makeup that may make you feel better equipped to step into group settings.

A Breakdown of Group Structure and Group Dynamics

To kick off our exploration of group interactions, let us first define what we mean by group structure. According to the American Psychological Association, group structure is *"the arrangement of individuals and their relationships, both implicit and formalized, in a group, including positions, roles, and patterns of authority, attraction, and communication."* I know—that is a lot to unpack! In the shortest possible terms, a group must be organized, or it will fall into chaos. This organization, in all its forms, is what we mean when we talk about group structure.

In any group, there are five different terms to consider:

1. **Roles.** A role describes the expected behaviors that someone in a group performs. In other words, if you behave a certain way in a group, you will be perceived in that way by everybody. A student, for instance, might be known as a funny and disruptive force by the rest of the class— this student is known as the class clown. When we talk about roles, we also talk about role perception, by exten-

sion, or the way in which everyone else sees a person's behavior. Your role in a group is largely influenced by role expectations or how the group believes you should act. Role conflict might arise when the behaviors or expectations of a role clash with those of another role.

Aside from the leader, there are several other common roles within professional and social groups. These include monitors *(those who encourage the group and defuse tension)*, note-keepers *(may summarize other people's points or ask lots of clarifying questions)*, and devil's advocates *(those who try to see both sides of every opinion)*. There are still dozens of unique roles that group members fill, depending on the context and needs of the group. Whenever you are in a group with unclear roles, it may be interesting to try to define what each group member's function might be.

2. **Norms.** In the most basic sense, norms are behaviors that a group finds acceptable, regardless of role or status. You are probably aware of the effect that norms have on one's behavior, in large part because of societal norms that we are taught when we are young *(chew food with your mouth closed, always say please and thank you, etc.)*. However, group norms can vary wildly depending on who you are with. Culture, background, physical setting, and existing group relationships can all be determining factors in group norms. The worst part about norms is that they are almost never explicitly stated. When you walk into a house party, your host probably will not hand you a list of accepted behaviors. For people who already have trouble navigating social situations, figuring out group norms can be a huge detractor from the experience of group socialization. To make matters worse, there are several different categories of norms. Some common examples include performance norms *(how people should perform at work)*, appearance norms

(how you should look), and social arrangement norms *(how its members should interact)*. Endearing yourself in a new group and building rapport ultimately means that you need to figure out the group's norms and conform to them as quickly as possible. Closely observing how people act and behave is a great way to establish what the group's norms might be, but you can also simply ask if you are unsure. Something along the lines of *"I am sorry, but is it all right if I…?"* is a great way to respect the norms of the group you are in.

3. **Status.** Existing both in the social world and the professional world, status is your official or unofficial ranking relative to other members in a group. Status implies the existence of a hierarchy that the group conforms to, and figuring out the hierarchy at play is a wise move. In general, leaders of groups tend to have a higher status than everyone else, followed by particularly valuable or insightful members. In professional situations, status is usually made clear to new group members, typically by titles like junior, associate, or senior.

4. **Cohesiveness.** This refers to how well people get along with each other in the professional and commercial spheres. Both in excess and in scarcity, group cohesiveness can present a difficult problem for members, leaders, and superiors in the workplace. On one end of the spectrum, a group gets along so well that they all become best friends… And get no work done. On the other end of the spectrum, group members get along so poorly with each other that, again, no work is done. In this arena, the ideal group is cohesive enough to be friendly but not so cohesive as to ignore work.

Understanding these forces will allow you to better categorize and define how a particular group works. From here, you can start looking at group dynamics to see the details of how people interact with each other. Typically, the tone for the rest of the group is set by the leader and can come in three different styles.

Authoritarian leadership is effectively a dictatorship for whatever group you are in. While the leader may not have had a direct hand in deciding the group's goals, they still have total control over exactly how that goal is accomplished. Leaders with an authoritarian style are usually more formal with their members, as well as more strict with the norms of the group. These leaders determine and enforce roles, norms, and size and often reserve the ability to award consequences to nonconforming group members. Authoritarian leaders make decisions without consulting the group and will usually provide exact details of their expectations. In short, leaders with a more authoritarian style believe in the adage, *"It is my way or the highway."*

Democratic leaders are the opposite of authoritarian leaders. This style of leadership consults the group's members at every turn, making sure that everyone has a role in determining the best course of action for any given mission. Under these leaders, group members generally have more leeway when it comes to group norms, behaviors, and roles, and they also tend to be somewhat less formal. Rather than forcing members to face the consequences directly from them, they will let the other members of the group determine what is acceptable and what is not. Democratic leadership styles tend to agree with the consensus of the group, sometimes even when it is against their own personal beliefs.

Finally, laissez-faire leaders are the most hands-off of the three. Rather than engaging with the group members, these types of leaders tend to let the group members figure everything out for themselves. Laissez-faire leadership is essentially an oxymoron, as these leaders do not really perform any leadership functions.

Group Communication Tips

Knowing all these definitions and structures, what can you do with all this information in a practical sense? Well, the basic principles of group communication that we have discussed previously still stand. Things like observing carefully, reading the room, gauging how much you speak, and knowing the right time to speak are all good starting points. However, one of the biggest things that you can do in a big, professional group is clarify your message.

Clarifying your message can be difficult, as big groups do not really give you the room to explain or extrapolate the things you want to showcase about yourself. When you speak, remember that you are speaking to several different people. In the interest of respecting their time and attention, you will want to make your message and delivery as clean as possible on the first try. Some things you can do to accomplish this include:

- **Speak slower than you normally would, and speak loud enough so that everyone in the group can hear you the first time.** The following phrases are widely regarded as an introvert's worst nightmare: *"Speak up!"* and *"I cannot hear you!"* can trigger a sinking feeling in your gut. To avoid this, make sure to increase the volume of your voice by using more air when you speak. While you do not have to enunciate every sound in every word, you want to talk a little bit slower than you normally would so that everyone has a chance to process your message.

- **Think about your message before you start speaking.** Another nightmare for introverts comes when you think you have gotten all your thoughts together, but every word still vacates your mind the second that a group is paying attention to you. Before you speak up, think about what you are trying to get across.

- **Be concise in your word choice.** The point you try to convey in a conversation can easily get lost if you use a lot of filler words. As much as you can, avoid phrases like *"Umm…"*, *"like,"* *"you know,"* and *"totally."* These phrases usually take up unnecessary space and make your message less interesting to listen to. In places where you really want to use a filler word, try taking a breath before you start speaking again.

At some point, you will end up stumbling over your words when you speak to big groups. A couple of jumbled words will not destroy your career or business. Occasionally stumbling over your words is perfectly normal in all kinds of conversations, and it is nothing to feel embarrassed about. Likely, no one will even remember when or how you misspoke. The important thing is to ground yourself in the reality of the situation—as long as you get back on your feet and keep trying to interact; you are doing just fine!

The way in which you communicate in big groups is certainly important, but your core message is just as vital. Here is where the concept of a value proposition comes into play. Communicating your value proposition effectively is the key to building your business, advancing your career, and making yourself an appealing social figure. As such, some kind of value proposition should be tied to your conversational hook in all situations. We will tackle the world of value propositions and how you can integrate yours into all your social, professional, and commercial interactions next.

CHAPTER 2

VALUE PROPOSITION

....

D o not get me wrong—relationships that are purely transactional can put your mental and emotional health in a state of disarray. Transactional relationships, at their core, focus only on what you can get out of another person or what another person can get out of you. This can be a completely disheartening idea, especially if you are an introvert looking to form new connections in your life. At the end of the day, we are people, not commodities. We seek out relationships with people for more than just achieving material benefit, and you should not let yourself fall into the trap of prioritizing transactions over genuine connections.

There is an undeniable reality in relationships that can be difficult to come to terms with. Ask yourself: *Why are you seeking out new social, professional, or commercial connections?* Sure, having a network of people for support is certainly a factor in your conversational journey. On the material side of the equation, however, you might also want:

- To gain from other people's knowledge or wisdom
- To attract monetary support for your business
- To have someone to be around when you do not want to be alone

In short, there are material benefits that you seek out in the people you speak with. In case you have not realized by now, there are plenty of people who are doing the exact same thing! In the interest of getting the material benefits that you want, you need to reciprocate by showing people what benefits you offer as a connection.

What Is Value Proposition?

At its core, your value proposition is made up of all the things that you bring to the table, from business connections and expertise to personal characteristics. In other words, everything that makes you an appealing person to strangers can be considered your value proposition. Of course, what you bring to the table may depend on what table you are sitting at.

Social Value Propositions

Socially, your value proposition is typically made up of things like your personality, your hobbies, your traits, and your emotional intelligence. Your social value proposition may also consist of your soft skills, like responsibility or empathy. Out of all your different value propositions, your personal and social value proposition is likely going to be the hardest to develop and communicate. In essence, you are putting together a shortlist of everything that makes you...well, you! While other value propositions may rely on certifications, metrics, or accomplishments, your personal value proposition is not contingent on any outside factors. Rather, your social value proposition is what you believe to be the best parts of yourself. If a stranger were to approach you, *what parts of your personality and character would be the most socially appealing to them?*

Determining your social value proposition is difficult enough, but communicating it to others will likely be even harder. To make it easier for yourself, try writing down a list of everything you like about your personality. These traits do not have to be big or flashy. Things as simple as punctuality or basic politeness are awesome qualities to have in a social relationship, especially as that relationship matures over time. In addition to your personality and traits, jot down some cool nonwork-related skills or passions of yours. *Are you an awesome baker? Do you go hiking every weekend?* When you find the right social connections, even the smallest of your hobbies can translate into social and emotional benefits for your conversational partners.

Professional Value Propositions

In the professional world, you are probably more used to seeing your value proposition in different formats. Your resume, cover letters, and even your professional elevator pitch can all tie into your overall value proposition. Basically, your goal here is to do the same thing you did with your social value proposition. Making a comprehensive list of everything you have to offer in the professional realm is a great start, and then you can narrow down the most appealing attributes from there.

According to one Forbes article, employers and professionals in your field are not just looking for hard skills and metrics. Rather, employers and businesses prefer more well-rounded candidates that balance four key factors; Material offerings, the potential for growth, a sense of community, and meaning or purpose. In the process of making your list, try to come up with at least a couple of bullet points for each of these areas. Just like with your social value proposition, try to come up with ways to show your value rather than simply relaying it to your audience. Showing the professional impact you have made in a company—through things like metrics, increased business, and money saved—is a great way to do this, and these bite-sized pieces of information are also easy to drop into professional conversations.

Commercial Value Propositions

By far the most popular option for value propositions, your commercial success depends entirely on your ability to outline the value of your product, brand, or business. While commercial value propositions follow the same general outline as other propositions (making a comprehensive list of your value sources and showing your audience what this means for them), there are a couple of things you might want to change as you go through the process. First, commercial value propositions are not necessarily focused on selling a person. Rather, commercial propositions require you to focus on your brand or your business, making the process a little farther removed from you as a person.

Because this is different from your professional and social value propositions, you may find that these steps result in a better commercial value proposition:

1. Outline all the benefits that your customer will see when they choose your product. While you want to be comprehensive, you also want to try to keep your value proposition concise.
2. Keep things short overall, and try not to go into too much detail.
3. As you create your value proposition, think about what your customer is going to think. Putting yourself in their shoes might give you a better insight into what they are looking for in a product.

Here, you can afford to be a little less personal when it comes to talking about benefits. In this situation, you are not trying to convince customers of your personal worth or professional accomplishments. As a result, you may find that talking about your commercial value proposition is much easier.

Indirect Communication Versus Direct Communication

When it comes to incorporating your value proposition into your conversations, not all contexts are created equal. For instance, you will find that more social and casual situations require a more indirect approach. Directly saying *"I am a fun-loving person"* to your partner is a little strange, and it may sound sarcastic in some instances. In order to show your partner the traits that you want, you will have to do just that—show, do not tell. If you want to come off as a fun-loving person, list activities that you engage in that might be considered fun-loving *("I tried indoor sky-diving last week, it was super fun!")*.

Meanwhile, direct communication of value propositions is more suited to professional or formal situations. In situations like interviews, for instance, you want to clearly state your accomplishments and hard skills in plain English. While showing your professional and commercial accomplishments is still a great idea, you should also make sure that your audience understands your qualifications. For example, you do not really want to beat around the bush when it comes to skills like CPR. Taking an indirect approach by saying that you have saved dozens of lives should come *after* direct communication. Similarly, things like degrees, coursework, certification, and licenses are all things that you should communicate clearly and directly.

Speaking With Intention

Chatting with coworkers by the coffee machine is great, but be aware that conversations always need to have a purpose. Transactional relationships can be toxic and unhealthy, but there is still an element of transactionalism in all our relationships. Similarly, purely transactional conversations can be draining and mentally taxing, but all conversations have some likeness to a transaction. As such, having a purpose for your interactions with people will make it easier to converse and socialize. On a general level, this purpose might look more like your conversational hook or the overarching theme that guides your long-term conversational goals. When we talk about value proposition, though, communicating your value proposition may become your primary goal in a conversation.

For some conversations, it is easy to make your intentions clear. Formal situations such as interviews or performance reviews essentially have your value proposition built into them, which makes it easy to advocate for yourself. In more casual and social contexts, accomplishing this goal becomes somewhat more difficult, particularly for those who are not used to communicating indirectly. In these types of situations, remember that you are not trying to "sell" yourself to your audience, per se. As you know, people tend to be good at spotting inauthenticity and dishonesty, and "selling" yourself in a conventional way might leave people with an unfavorable impression of you. When you sell something, you become a salesman. People who are salesmen of themselves are not always pleasant to be around, and their interactions can easily devolve into one-sided conversations.

Instead of becoming a conversational salesman, try approaching your value proposition from a more personable and authentic angle. Showing rather than telling can accomplish this, but make sure that you are not dominating the conversation with accomplishments or qualities. When chances to show your value proposition arises, drop breadcrumbs for the other person to pick up on. Rattling off all the details on your resume is boring to sit through, so choose two or three main points to focus on in every conversation.

Research Your Topic and Subject

When you start asserting your value proposition in conversations, there are a few things you can do that can boost your chances for success. Researching the context of the conversation beforehand is always a great move, and it comes in handy for narrowing down which aspects of your value proposition you want to focus on. You basically want your value proposition to match the situation you are in. If you were attending a charity event, for instance, a good value proposition might emphasize your commitment to philanthropic causes and your empathy. From here, you can chat with people about other charities you like, why the charity's mission matters to you, or how you discovered the organization. You *do not* want to seem like you are boasting, so stay away from talking about things like monetary donations you have made. In addition to the overall context of your conversation, try to research the types of people you will be talking to as well. Getting a sense of people's personal values will give you a leg up when you present your value proposition, and you will be able to align yourself with them. Social media can be a good method for this kind of personal research, but word-of-mouth information from people you know tends to be better. Moreover, you do not want to initiate a conversation with a person only to realize that you have no idea what you are talking about. If, say, you attend a networking event for jobseekers in software engineering, you should know about software engineering. Speaking to people about areas you do not know well is a recipe for disaster, so make sure that you research the actual content of what you will be discussing. Between researching the setting, people, and content of the interaction, you should be able to gain some insight into how to present your value proposition.

We have talked previously about speaking confidently in conversations, but this can be a very daunting thing if you are not a stereotypically confident or loud person. Let's now take a deep dive into all things confidence—how to build mental confidence through conversations, how to instill confidence in other people, and how to physically convey confidence to your conversational partner.

CHAPTER 3

BEING CONFIDENT AND ASSERTIVE

....

T he term "confidence" can define a wide array of things. Its meaning depends largely on the context of a situation and the source of your information, and certain uses of the word can occasionally do more harm than good.

Confidence is not really associated with introversion, and this is because surface-level confidence relies on things like volume, gregariousness, and sociability. When we think of confident people, we might think of those who excel in social situations or those who can somehow talk to everyone comfortably. Confidence is much deeper than simply speaking more than everyone else. The Oxford Dictionary defines confidence as *"a feeling of self-assurance arising from one's appreciation of one's own abilities or qualities,"* and this definition is probably what you had typically expected of someone who is stereotypically confident. While this can certainly be the case for some people, I prefer Oxford's secondary and tertiary definitions: *"the state of feeling certain about the truth of something"* and *"the feeling or belief that one can rely on someone or something; firm trust."*

Introverts find natural socialization to be a little bit uncomfortable, which makes the typical meaning of confidence feel more out of reach. However, quiet confidence is attainable for those who are willing, to be honest, authentic, and steadfast.

Building Confidence, Both Inside and Outside

For introverts, who internalize the world, you do not really have to change anything about yourself to start building confidence. For you, the confidence-building process will start on the inside. Self-confidence, as with externalized confidence, starts with being honest with yourself. Grounding yourself is crucial to understanding yourself, your achievements, and your inherent value, and strong self-confidence is a major aspect of good communication.

In the last chapter, you drew up a list of your achievements, qualities, and characteristics for your professional and social value propositions. For many, acknowledging all these things was probably a little uncomfortable. In fact, the mere practice of doing this is a step toward self-confidence. To build yourself up, you need to acknowledge your worth regularly. So, your self-confidence routine will start with a similar method of list-making:

- **Acknowledging your worth.** More than simply writing down a list of skills, acknowledging your worth stems from really sitting down and thinking about what you do well. In terms of building self-confidence, thinking about specific times when you have felt proud or accomplished is a more meaningful way to recognize your value. In this case, you do not want to just rattle off all the things that are on your resume. Instead, focus on what you genuinely, truly believe are the best traits, skills, and characteristics in your toolbox.

- **Stopping your inner critic in its tracks.** Feeling confident about your abilities is not enough. To become more confident *(and stay confident in the long term),* you also need to know how to stop yourself from backtracking. Grounding yourself in the reality of a situation may work for some, but your inner critic probably will not stop there. When you start doubting yourself or your abilities, catch those thoughts as they cross your mind. Remember, these thoughts are not a true reflection, and nor are they what you really think or feel—self-deprecating feelings come from your inner critic, which is separate from the real you. You and your inner critic are going to be at odds most of the time, and this is okay. Instead of listening to your inner critic, try treating yourself as you had treated a stranger, with an objective perspective and compassion.

- **Adopt a mentality of equality.** Oftentimes, we go into situations thinking that other people are better than us in some way, even if they are strangers whom we have never met before. In reality, of course, everyone has their own unique strengths and weaknesses, and it is nearly impossible to judge people accurately without getting to know them well. Chances are, you are not all that different from the person you are speaking with. Outside of static status roles like those you had found in a workplace, try to view yourself and others as peers. This will start breaking down the you-versus-them mentality, and it will also allow you to converse more comfortably.

There is a lot of inner work that accompanies self-confidence, and it can sometimes take a lot for people to develop that skill. In the meantime, you should still learn to speak to people with confidence, even if you are a quieter person.

As we said before, not all forms of confidence are created equal. For some, confidence looks like having an outgoing or gregarious personality, while others may find more utility in displaying quiet confidence. Quiet confidence, unlike the typical definition of confidence, does not rely on being a social butterfly. Instead, try doing things like:

- Accepting the possibility of making mistakes or being wrong

- Speaking up for your needs and the needs of others
- Taking calculated risks
- Actively listening to everyone in a situation
- Speaking slowly and clearly

These are all subtle ways that you can show your confidence. Additionally, self-trust is a big aspect of confidence. Before you go into conversational situations, take some time to say a couple of affirmations. Phrases like *"No matter what happens, I know that I will figure it out"* and *"My worth is not tied to my professional success"* can really help boost your sense of self.

Know the Jargon of Professional Spaces

In professional and commercial contexts, nothing says confidence like competence. Competence in the business world is communicated largely through jargon, though professionals must be careful not to overuse or underuse jargon.

When it comes to word choice in formal settings, there are a few common-sense things to avoid, like using profanities or slang, gossiping, or being disrespectful. Using people's correct names and titles, proper grammar, and a professional tone is all standard in workplaces, and you should try to stick to typical business etiquette. If you are new to a space, however, jargon can often present an interesting obstacle. In situations where professionals might use jargon, conducting research beforehand is key. Common jargon for your industry or company can be easily found online and through places like:

- LinkedIn
- Indeed
- Job boards and forums
- Professional resources like papers, studies, blogs, or articles

Once you have a handle on some common industry terms, do not be afraid to make a glossary for yourself to refer to, either digitally or physically. Something like a sticky note on your computer might even be enough to learn common vernacular for your industry.

Failing to use any jargon at all may implicitly communicate your unfamiliarity with a subject to others. However, using jargon all the time is a worse offense. Oftentimes, industry jargon uses buzzwords—fashionable words or phrases that usually stem from cultural movements—that can cloud or distill the actual meaning of what you are trying to say. This buzzword-jargon crossover can make people sound dismissive, incompetent, and even rude. In the general business world, terms like value-added, sustainability, financial bandwidth, retargeting, alignment, or synergy constitute buzzword jargon. Similarly, acronyms can also fall into this category, especially if the acronym itself is unclear. To make things even worse, this buzzword-jargon combination usually changes depending on what is going on in society, making the game of word choice more tiresome to keep up with.

On a practical level, though, what is the danger of jargon at work? According to clinical business communication professor Peter Cardon, buzzword-jargon and the use of big words can work against you in a very real way: *"The first impression is that [the speaker] is trying to sound impressive... People are processing the information in real-time. If they do not know what a term means, you can lose someone in a moment."* You do not want your audience to have to stop and look up what a word means, and you do not want to inundate them with socially or politically charged buzzwords. All in all, stick to the basics—as with most communication in professional arenas, use direct communication and say what you mean as concisely as possible. In turn, this will leave others with the impression that you are both competent in your field and confident in your message.

Give Information Freely

Professional, commercial, and social confidence also necessitates that you trust your conversational partner. You do not have to share your life's secrets or regrets—in fact, this would be unfavorable—but you should still endeavor to open up to them in a personable and informative way. Doing so will make you seem open, engaged, and secure in your sense of self.

In professional contexts, you should try to share *(but not overshare)*. You want to impart interesting knowledge and know-how to your colleagues and peers, but you do not want to talk their ears off or bore them with information-dense conversations. As always, wait for the right opportunity to deliver information, and do not try to force your information onto the center stage of a conversation. Stay away from unsolicited advice, and make sure to only talk about areas that you are knowledgeable in.

Speaking about information, both personal and professional, that is unique to you is crucial in conveying confidence to an audience. Sometimes, however, speaking with confidence becomes difficult when your audience gets bigger. So far, we have been talking about conversations in dyads and groups, *but what about professional presentations in front of crowds?* In the next book, we will go over the basics of public speaking, as well as some tips and tricks to feel more comfortable on stage.

Book 5:
Engaging and Persuasive Communication

Small Talk, Big Impact - The Power of
Everyday Conversations to Persuade and Connect

Kirsten Rae Evans

TABLE OF CONTENTS

INTRODUCTION

In your commercial and professional life, you probably know several people whom you consider to be master communicators. They are fascinating to observe, and the information they have is unique and one-of-a-kind. These people may be individuals that you know personally, like bosses or mentors, or they may be people that you have never met, like industry experts or presenters. Whatever relationship you have with them, one thing is certain—you enjoy watching them speak.

For folks who are quieter, this may seem like a complete mystery. *How can a person captivate an audience so completely? How do master communicators prepare for this kind of communication?* As you watch them move and speak, you may begin to think about the mechanics of how they do what they do. Of course, there is a wealth of research that pours into these very questions and hundreds of academic articles that study the relationship between audiences and engaging speakers. There are plenty of physiological and psychological reasons why we find good speakers engaging. For our purposes, we will examine three core areas that indicate mastery of communication: Leadership communications, persuasion, and storytelling.

CHAPTER 1

ADDRESSING CROWDS
AND BIG AUDIENCES

A fear of public speaking is one of the most common things that introverts (and almost everyone else) face, both in the workplace and otherwise. According to Orai, a public speaking consulting company, nearly three-quarters (77%) of the population in the U.S. experience at least some anxiety around public speaking. While most people are nervous before they get up on stage, anxiety levels may be different between different people. People who prefer to internalize information are usually less inclined to want to present information to large audiences, and introverts may also experience higher levels of anxiety as a result.

Some of the fear that accompanies public speaking stems from simply being observed. Even if you are an expert in your field, the feeling of having tens or dozens of people watching you speak can be disconcerting. Additionally, unlike typical conversations, speaking to a crowd has a very clear structure: A presenter speaks to a crowd, and everyone in the crowd listens. This places all the pressures of a normal conversation *(providing valuable information, keeping people engaged, using the right word choice)* on one person.

Even if you are in a professional position that requires speaking to large audiences as a presenter, it is still natural to feel some stage fright. Knowing a bit more about the relationship between you and your audience might help alleviate some of the nervousness you face.

Audience Dynamics

Unlike big, interactive group conversations, speaking to crowds only involves two main roles; a presenter and the audience. As a presenter, you are going to be outnumbered by your audience, which makes it important to understand the dynamics at play in your audience. In essence, audience dynamics describes everything that influences the behavior of the audience members, like motivations, attitudes, values, and opinions.

Hopefully, you are already aware of the fact that you cannot really change people's motivations or core values—inevitably, people are going to hear you and have a negative response because of their preexisting beliefs. Your message might sway the opinions of your audience, but at the end of the day, you cannot control other people. Rather than worrying about what you cannot control when it comes to presenting, worry about all the things that you *can* control. Tailoring your message and delivery to your audience is the best thing you can do, and this process starts with research. In short, you need to find out everything you can about who your audience is, what their motivations are, and how to effectively communicate with them. In this way, presenting in a professional capacity is a lot like conducting market research for a product. Some entry-level research you can do includes things like looking at industry reports, case studies, and formal research papers that are like what you are going to be discussing. This is yet another instance where leveraging your professional connections comes in handy—if you have peers or colleagues that have dealt with this type of audience before, or if they themselves are a member of this audience, ask them about how best to get your point across. On a smaller level, looking at social media trends can be a great way to gauge where your audience stands on topics.

From here, you will get a rough sketch of what your audience looks like in terms of motivations and beliefs. You can flesh out this sketch by doing multiple rounds of research before you get up on stage, creating a fuller picture of the audience you will be working with. At this point, there are a few things to keep in mind:

- **Do not make assumptions or leap to conclusions about what your audience will respond to.** As with everything you do professionally, you should have some form of proof that backs up your claims.
- **If you are still unsure about how to communicate effectively, look at other presenters and their methods of communication.** Seeing different presenters in action can give you some helpful insight into what presenting looks like in real-time.
- **You do not have to commit only to one way of presenting.** If you find that another method of communication works better, do not hesitate to switch things up.
- **Integrate unique insights and knowledge into your presentation.** If your audience wanted by-the-book information, they would have done a quick Google search. Rather, they are looking for you to keep them engaged as you share your information.
- **Speak directly to people, and do not get caught up in reading your notes.** Dynamic speakers do not just read from a page—your audience could do that themselves. Rather, talk as if there wasn't a page in front of you, and make sure to only look at your resources when you really need to.

Presenting in front of a crowd can be a difficult thing to master. It is not the only situation in which you might need to speak in front of a bigger audience, though. Interacting with presenters, speaking in more dynamic group meetings, and other formal meetings sometimes also require you to address a large group. In these situations, the pressure is somewhat lower, given that you are not forced to speak the entire time. However, the rules for presenting still apply to these other forms of public speaking.

How to Talk to Many People Confidently

In addition to the content of your presentation, you should also be aware of your delivery. Speaking calmly and slowly, taking deep breaths, and standing or sitting up straight are basic things that convey confidence to your audience, but presenters usually must worry about a bit more than the basics.

In terms of posture, a lot of speakers present their material standing up, sometimes without a podium. In these cases, you should remember that it is all right to move around a bit more. Standing in one spot with a perfectly straight posture for the entirety of your presentation can get a bit boring to watch for your audience members, so slowly walking around may work to engage your listeners more. Another hurdle is sound quality and microphones. If you are working with a handheld microphone, you want to make sure that you are speaking close enough to the microphone to be heard but not so close that the sound is difficult to listen to. Prior to your presentation, do a quick sound check to make sure that everything is working properly. Alternatively, you might be presenting material without a microphone. In this case, it is even more important that you speak loudly and clearly so that every audience member can hear you. Using your hands while talking is a good idea, but make sure not to move too much, as this can distract your listeners. Try not to touch your face, put your hands in your pockets, or put your hands on your hips. For those who tend to fidget, it can be helpful to hold something small while you talk, like a pen.

Regarding visual cues, you have a few options. Presentations may be done with a simple note sheet that you bring with you, or you could present with a slideshow. As with paper notes, make sure that you never read from your slideshow unless you are reading a direct quote from someone. In terms of design, you also want your slideshow to be simple and minimalistic. In essence, you want your audience to focus more on what you are saying than what they are seeing in the PowerPoint. Visual cues should support your content, not distract from it!

As always, mental preparation before speaking to people is key. Presenting is no different, and it may take you a few run-throughs before you start to feel comfortable with your content and delivery. While it may feel strange, try delivering your presentation in front of a mirror or in front of someone you trust. This will allow you to practice your material in a safe space while simultaneously getting used to seeing a face while you present. At the end of the day, it is important to remember that there is no such thing as a perfect presentation. Presentations, like all other conversations, are dynamic and versatile, and you may have to change and adapt as you speak. Luckily, your audience does not expect perfection. Before you start feeling self-conscious about your presentation, recall your audience's motivation for listening to you. By prioritizing the reason for the presentation, the pressure on you is lessened.

Addressing Subordinates

If you are presenting material or speaking to large crowds regularly, there is a good chance that you are in a position of professional seniority. Dealing with subordinates at work is a little bit different from dealing with peers or superiors, and knowing how to be an effective leader is the key to advancing your career. We initially talked about the concept of cohesion in a group and how groups that are overly cohesive or lacking cohesion tend to be less productive. This is doubly true for those in managerial or leadership positions. In other words, you want to create a welcoming space for your subordinates, but you still want to maintain a professional hierarchy.

People who are more introverted may struggle with this idea, especially given that you will not be able to be friends with everyone. Walking the line between groups that are too cohesive and groups that are not cohesive is fraught with pitfalls, and a big part of your job is figuring out how to communicate effectively with your team. While this will look different for everyone, here are some good starting points for effective communication with subordinates:

- **Encourage feedback and make yourself approachable.** Phrases like *"My door is always open"* and *"Feel free to reach out with questions"* are a good way to communicate this. You should also endeavor to follow through on your commitments to subordinates by keeping your door open, so to speak. If someone brings up legitimate feedback or even critiques, make sure to listen carefully!
- **Communicate with your subordinates clearly and consistently.** We have all had bosses who do not tell us what is going on. This is not an ideal way to work, and you should try to relay new information to your team as soon as you receive it.
- **Use the right channels for your message.** In-person and online meetings can be great for discussing problems, but keep in mind that other formats may be better for smaller pieces of information. If you can send information via email or Slack instead of a meeting, this will free up your subordinates' time for productivity.
- **Get to know your subordinates personally.** To understand how your subordinates work best, you need to get to know them individually. More casual one-on-one meetings are excellent for this purpose, and you should

136

conduct these types of meetings regularly with all your subordinates.

- **Use active listening.** When someone from your team comes to you with a problem, it is your job to find some kind of resolution, whether it is readjusting expectations, giving advice, or delegating. Make sure that you understand the problems that your team faces, and try your best to keep morale up by showing genuine care and attention.

As with all conversations, always speak to people respectfully. If you treat your subordinates well, they will reward you by being productive. Sometimes, you will need to take on even more of a leadership role when things at work do not go to plan. Talking about the future, managing expectations, and dealing with resistance from subordinates are all common issues that arise in the professional sphere. In these instances, you will need a couple more tools to communicate efficiently and effectively.

CHAPTER 2

COMMUNICATE LIKE A LEADER

....

U nfortunately, we cannot always accurately predict the problems that can arise in a workplace. From global pandemics to international conflicts, there are a plethora of things that can affect the nature of your work, the professional contexts in which you find yourself, and the way you communicate. The COVID-19 pandemic is a clear example of this, and the pandemic also deeply affected the way that we connect with each other. In 2019, Zoom hosted 10 million people per day. This number leaped up to 300 million by 2020. Professionals were suddenly thrust into a completely different work situation, which ultimately forced them to adjust their communication methods.

Good leaders work hard to make sure that everyone in the workplace receives accurate and current information. While we cannot see what the future holds, we can take steps to mitigate risks and improve our methods of professional communication.

Addressing the Future

Talking about the future with subordinates is tricky, in large part because the future is uncertain. It is one thing to know that something is coming, but it is another thing entirely to plan for the unexpected. As a result, leaders and professionals need a generalized framework for dealing with issues as they arise. The shortest game plan in any situation is effectively composed of two steps: Identify and prepare.

In situations where you know what the problem is, you are already halfway done. In more unclear situations, on the other hand, you may need to identify several potential problems and their consequences. This list of potential problems can include any change that your industry faces, any change within your company, and even changes within your team or group. Things like mergers, lacking employee performance, and changes in leadership can all turn into major concerns, so you should plan for them as best you can. As you make your list, think about the consequences of events, as well as changes that have occurred in similar industries or companies. Next, you need to plan for each situation. Lacking employee performance, for instance, requires things like periodic performance checks, in-depth conversations with the employee in question, and providing resources for improvement. No matter what the situation may be, all your communications with your team should happen early and often, more so than normal.

As you prepare for conversations about uncertain futures, consider things like:

- The needs and perspectives of your audience
- Keeping your communications consistent throughout the uncertainty
- Changing or maintaining performance standards

When tough situations arise, you never want to sugarcoat your conversations. Continuing to be authentic, honest, and empathetic towards your subordinates will be greatly appreciated, even if turbulence occurs. In your communications, do not be afraid to offer support to subordinates during hard times, and remember to listen to their concerns carefully.

The Art of Persuasive Communication

Sometimes, situations in the workplace require you to put in some extra effort when it comes to communicating. Not everyone will agree with you, and sometimes your peers, subordinates, and superiors will try to simply override your input. In most situations, flexing the power or status that you have is the wrong move. This style of leadership communication is called authoritarian leadership, but it is not limited to people in formal leadership positions. Conducting yourself in this way can put people on edge, ruin professional relationships that you have built, and paint you as a workplace villain. Instead, you need to lean into your soft skills to convey the importance of your arguments.

How can you persuade people who staunchly disagree with you? This is a question that every leader and professional grapple with, and many have reached different conclusions as to the best approach. At the core of your techniques, you have two options; you can implement either a positive reinforcement, which promises rewards for desired behavior, or a negative reinforcement, which promises consequences for negative behavior. At first, positive reinforcements are the primary way that you will convince people to agree with you. In other words, *"If you do X, Y, and Z, a good thing will happen."* This will typically result in better outcomes, and you should only turn to negative reinforcements as a last resort. Going deeper, you can use multi-faceted appeals through ethos, logos, and pathos. Ethos, or your credibility, can be used to make people feel that you know what you are doing. Logos, or the logic of your appeal, relies on the fact that your point of view is objectively reasonable. Pathos, or an emotional appeal, relies on motivating your audience to agree with you because of their emotions.

Additionally, your persuasion is also served by considering the needs of your audience. You have probably heard of Maslow's hierarchy of needs, but let us refresh the order anyway. According to this hierarchy, people require (in order) physiological needs like food and shelter, safety needs, social needs, self-esteem needs, and self-actualization needs. Good persuasive arguments apply this hierarchy to people and determine need-based problems that they might face. If your peer disagrees with you at work, you could make an appeal to their self-actualization by claiming that your point of view will further their career. Before you make any appeals to your audience, try finding common ground that you can leverage. Making your point of view seem like a solution to a shared problem is a great tactic, as it presents both positive and negative reinforcements while putting you and your audience on the same side.

Sometimes, you simply will not be able to persuade people to see your point of view. At this point, it is usually best to document your attempts and move on. Whether you win people over or not, it is always important to prioritize your existing relationships over a single issue. Throughout your persuasive communications, you should always treat everyone with respect and dignity, especially those who disagree with you.

Presence Through Dominance and Prestige

When speaking to people in the workplace, you do not always have to be strongly assertive. Talking casually with a coworker does not really require any use of force or dominance, and being overly aggressive can really decrease your social and professional value proposition. Nobody likes to work with someone who is antagonistic or full of themselves! Unfortunately, there are a lot of sources out there that advise professionals to present themselves as completely dominant, which in turn implies that your subordinates, peers, and superiors are submissive. Oftentimes, this style of professional communication focuses too much on one's self and not enough on others. Maintaining a "me-versus-world" mentality will not garner you much professional favor, and it usually sets you up for failure.

This type of toxic dominance is not healthy behavior, and it is not what you want to convey to people. If you are in a leadership position, however, establishing your status as a leader *is* important in defining your work relationships. You want people to listen to what you say, and you want to use natural, healthy dominance to make your professional space better for everyone. In short—you need to develop a leadership presence.

According to one team of Canadian and British researchers, there are effectively two ways in which you can establish a strong leadership presence. Dominance, in their definition, is behavior that uses clear positive and negative reinforcements to motivate people. In practice, this looks like giving people raises for good work and using the threat of punishment to make sure that people are staying on task. Dominant leaders tend to "tell" rather than "show," and they also tend to communicate in a very direct manner. Prestige, on the other hand, is behavior that influences people with knowledge and extensive experience. This looks like the ethos, logos, and pathos arguments that we talked about earlier, with a heavy emphasis on ethos and logos appeals. Both approaches work, but the situations in which you use them will differ. Your presence as a leader—and by extension, the conversational approaches that you implement—is determined by your use of these two methods.

Dominance is best used when you and your subordinates have a clear goal. When things need to get done on time, when there are many moving pieces in a project, and when metrics are important, direct communication is preferred. In these situations, there is no room for anything that falls outside the scope of your group's mission. Prestige works better when you are trying to boost creativity or morale or when you have a bit more freedom to explore options. Leaders who opt for prestige usually care more about what others think, while leaders who opt for dominance care more about the bottom line. As a leader, you do not have to commit to just one approach. In fact, the best leaders often tend to use a combination of the two approaches.

Whether you are a leader, a junior employee, or a solo entrepreneur, establishing a leadership presence is a helpful step to take. When you have conversations with people, being viewed as someone with strong leadership skills can help you in the long run. Similarly, you also want to keep your conversational partners engaged when you speak. If you really want to enhance your leadership presence, storytelling is the best way to do it. Next, we will dive into the world of telling stories, from funny dinner party anecdotes to parables that you can use in your professional life.

CHAPTER 3

THE SCIENCE OF STORYTELLING

....

We are surrounded by stories. Books, shows, movies, podcasts, anecdotes, religious texts, and even our own stories are constantly repeating, even when we do not realize it. Telling stories, both to ourselves and to each other, is about as old as humanity! Stories make us care about their subjects, they connect us with each other, they teach us important lessons, and they convey the crux of what it means to be human.

Naturally, telling and listening to stories in all aspects of our lives is a beneficial thing. For introverts, however, crafting a good story and creating interest in a conversation presents a big challenge. If someone requested that you tell them a feel-good story right now, could you do it? Could you deliver the storyline in a meaningful, impactful, and engaging way? Could you construct a moral that teaches a lesson? For many of us, the answer is a resounding no. As much as we consume stories, telling one yourself can be a daunting task, especially if you are in a room full of expectant listeners. To understand how storytelling can be used in your conversations and to understand how to tell a great story, we need to break stories down into their component parts.

What Is a Story?

In essence, storytelling is a verbal representation of a journey of some kind. In every story, characters end in a different place than where they started, either physically or metaphorically, and change is a major element in good storytelling. This change can be triggered by obstacles, events, or interactions, and it is generally meant to convey something about life or human nature. Like a presentation, there are two parties involved in storytelling—a listener and a storyteller.

Stories are great devices for explaining complex information on a wide variety of subjects, making them versatile and easy to understand. Additionally, even though stories are mostly performed through oration, there are visual, kinesthetic, and auditory aspects of stories that make them memorable to different types of learners and communicators. At work, exchanging stories creates stronger bonds between professionals and can increase levels of empathy, compassion, and commitment to work. Physiologically, much of this is due to a process called neural coupling. Among many other complex processes in the brain, neural coupling triggers the release of dopamine, which allows both listeners and orators to relate more deeply with each other.

On a practical, everyday level, telling stories accomplishes several things, both personal and professional:

- Impacts your listeners and evokes emotional responses
- Encourages mentorship and increased levels of communication
- Creates common ground with peers and social equals
- Makes people trust you more
- Creates more opportunities for you to be authentic and vulnerable

How to Craft a Relevant Story

How, then, do we begin to tell meaningful stories? In most situations, you are going to want to tell fables. No, we do not mean fairy tales or legends. A fable is a story that ends with a moral or a lesson, and you will typically use this mode of storytelling to describe lessons that you have personally learned. The lessons at the end of your stories should relate back to either your motivation for having a conversation or your bigger thematic hook. Either way, you should have a motive for telling a story before you begin to relay it. Otherwise, there is a good chance that you will start rambling without any exit plan.

Let us take you as an example—yes, you! Your motivation for talking with people is to become a better conversationalist, at least in some capacity. This is the theme and/or moral of your story.

From here, there are several structures that you can choose from when you craft the details of your story. Unless you want to write a novel, it is best to stick to a simple two-step structure. The first part of your story presents some sort of challenge or obstacle, and the second part presents a response to that obstacle. When you are telling your story, it is best to opt for tales that are short and sweet. It is usually better to leave your audience wanting more than to make your story too long or boring. Try to bring in universally relatable elements, like waking up late in the morning or having a bad hair day. Whatever relatable element you use, make sure that it is something that everyone in your audience knows about or deals with regularly.

In your case, the challenge of your story is the difficulty you face when you interact with people. The response to that challenge is the steps you take to get better at having conversations.

From here, you can start creating the steps that your story will follow as you illustrate the narrator's journey. Things like additional conflicts, actions, or other developments are great ways to punctuate your narrative's challenge, but they should not cloud the overarching theme that you are trying to get at. Throughout these steps, you can add a handful of details that make your storytelling more engaging, like sensory details or funny quips. You can also add information about setbacks or other mini-challenges, as this will build suspense around the end of your story.

In your case, the steps of your journey are learning to break the ice, initiating conversations, keeping your conversations alive, and gradually branching into other forms of interaction. At this point, you are ready to tie all the elements in your story together and bring the tale to a close.

Ending the Story

As you finish telling your story, you do not necessarily need to state the moral explicitly. Rather, the characters or figures in the story should indicate what the moral is without having to elaborate. For example, think about the fable about the tortoise and the hare—the infamous moral of the story can be summarized as "slow and steady wins the race," or the idea that taking the time to do things right is often the best option. In the tale, the tortoise and the hare are metaphors for different approaches to the same problem. This allows us to clearly see the moral without needing additional explanation. While your stories do not need to include personified animals, using characters or challenges as allegories is a great way to get your point across.

In most, if not all, stories that you tell in conversations, you should try to end on a positive or hopeful note. Going back to the tortoise and the hare, the story ends happily when the tortoise wins the race, despite being the slower competitor. Similarly, you should have the hero of your story win, even if the hero is a concept or an approach rather than a literal person. Another great ending to a story is the implication of the hero's future or the use of the future tense. We all know the stereotypical fairy tale ending "...and they all lived happily ever after", and while it is a bit exaggerated, it still exudes a positive sentiment.

Again, you do not want to drag out your ending or explain your story's moral too much. Rather, let your audience read between the lines and figure out what you mean. If you have told the story well, they will see your meaning without any help from you.

CONCLUSION

B y now, you have gone through the entire journey of a conversation—from icebreakers that you can keep in your back pocket to building rapport that lasts beyond the end of the conversation. You now have useful tools for mental preparation at your disposal, like affirmations, research, and understanding your motivations behind initiating conversations. You have also developed a conversational hook or the explicit reason why you are talking with someone. When in a conversation, you now have several approaches that you can try, depending on the context. These include:

- Asking good questions and following up after your partner is done responding
- Creating a good first impression through mirroring
- Using the proper word choice, vernacular, and delivery for the situation
- Changing the scenery of the conversation and hinting at future conversations

We also explored when and how to address groups of people, whether at networking events, dinner parties, or group interviews. In professional and commercial roles, we explained how to best present material to a crowd, as well as how to keep a crowd engaged. In the professional sphere, we went over how to establish your leadership presence through dominance and prestige, how to deal with uncertainty, and how to persuade people. Finally, you learned how to tell your story, along with creating an effective moral.

The journey to becoming a better conversationalist is never over. The intricacies of things like body language, gestures, and other nonverbal modes of communication are complicated, and it takes a lot of time and energy to refine your skills. However, a conversation is completely and totally within your grasp. Now, all that is left to do is go out and start interacting with the world around you!

GLOSSARY

1. **Audience Dynamics:** Motivations, attitudes, values, and opinions that influence the behavior of your audience.

2. **Authoritarian Leadership Style:** A totalitarian approach wherein a group leader determines a group's goals, member roles, norms, and consequences.

3. **Democratic Leadership Style:** A leadership approach that prioritizes the input of other group members in the pursuit of a goal.

4. **Dominance:** A leadership approach that is direct, efficient, and uses both positive and negative reinforcements to motivate employees and subordinates.

5. **Expressive Leadership:** A leadership approach that is relationship-oriented and prioritizes group harmony over group goals.

6. **Group Cohesiveness:** How well the members of a group get along with each other socially.

7. **Group Norms:** A set of behaviors that a group determines to be acceptable.

8. **Group Roles:** A set of expected behaviors that are performed by one person in a group, typically tied to a professional or social function.

9. **Group Status:** The official or unofficial ranking of members in a group, based on either a social or professional hierarchy.

10. **The Halo Effect:** A bias that transfers one's positive traits onto other unrelated areas of focus.

11. **Homophily:** The tendency for similarities between people who spend large amounts of time together.

12. **Hook:** The theme, motivation, or subject you use to guide your conversations.

13. **Instrumental Leadership:** A leadership approach that is goal-oriented and which prioritizes accomplishing a group's goals over the group's relationships.

14. **Laissez-Faire Leadership Style:** A leadership approach that lets the members of a group make most or all the decisions.

15. **Mirroring:** The act of subtly mimicking another's body language, expression, and vernacular.

16. **Prestige:** A leadership approach that is indirect, creative, and prioritizes wisdom and knowledge rather than force.

17. **Value Proposition:** A summary of why you, your professional skills, or your product is valuable to your audience.

REFERENCES

Abdulrahman, K. (2019). *Eight basic public speaking tips*. Entrepreneur. https://www.entrepreneur.com/en-ae/growth-strategies/eight-basic-public-speaking-tips/332948

Albright, L., Cohen, A. I., Malloy, T. E., Christ, T., & Bromgard, G. (2004). Judgments of communicative intent in conversation. *Journal of Experimental Social Psychology, 40*(3), 290–302. https://doi.org/10.1016/j.jesp.2003.06.004

Allan, P. (2015). *How to deal with someone who constantly rambles*. Lifehacker. https://lifehacker.com/how-to-deal-with-someone-who-constantly-rambles-1677630626

American Psychological Association. (2023). *APA dictionary of psychology*. Dictionary.apa.org. Retrieved May 21, 2023, from https://dictionary.apa.org/group-structure#:~:text=the%20arrangement%20of%20individuals%20and

Andersen, C. H. (2023). *125 Conversation starters that make you instantly interesting*. Reader's Digest. https://www.rd.com/list/conversation-starters/

Arizpe, S. (2023). *3 ways to lead during uncertainty*. Entrepreneur. https://www.entrepreneur.com/leadership/3-ways-to-lead-during-uncertainty/442806

Bailey, L. (2023). *The risks of having transactional relationships with your peers*. The Bailey Group Minneapolis. https://thebaileygroup.com/the-risks-of-having-transactional-relation-ships-with-your-peers/

Beheshti, N. (2018). *Are hard skills or soft skills more important to be an effective leader?* Forbes. https://www.forbes.com/sites/nazbeheshti/2018/09/24/are-hard-skills-or-soft-skills-more-important-to-be-an-effective-leader/?sh=522b39862eb3

Blank, A. (2021). *3 easy tips to help you communicate persuasively.* Forbes. https://www.forbes.com/sites/averyblank/2021/08/17/3-easy-tips-to-help-you-communicate-persuasively/

Boogaard, K. (2017). *7 habits of irresistibly engaging conversationalists.* Inc.com. https://www.inc.com/kat-boogaard/7-habits-of-irresistibly-engaging-conversationalists.html

Boogaard, K. (2017). *Here is how to cut off your rambling co-worker.* The Muse. https://www.themuse.com/advice/get-rambling-coworker-back-on-track

Boogaard, K. (2021). *An explanation of SMART goals and how to write them.* Work Life by Atlassian. https://www.atlassian.com/blog/productivity/how-to-write-smart-goals#:~:text=What%20are%20SMART%20goals%3F

Brooke, E. (2022). *The introvert's guide to actually enjoying a party.* Vox. https://www.vox.com/even-better/23297099/introvert-party-socializing-energy

Brooks, A. W., & John, L. K. (2018). *How to ask great questions.* Harvard Business Review. https://hbr.org/2018/05/the-surprising-power-of-questions

Brower, T. (2023). *For effective communication tone (surprise!) matters most: 5 strategies for effectiveness.* Forbes. https://www.forbes.com/sites/tracybrower/2023/02/26/for-effective-communication-tone-surprise-matters-most-5-strategies-for-effectiveness/

Brown, Z. C., Anicich, E. M., & Galinsky, A. D. (2021). *Does your office have a jargon problem?* Harvard Business Review. https://hbr.org/2021/03/do-you-have-a-jargon-problem

Brustein, D. (2017). *The 55 best questions to ask to break the ice and really get to know someone.* Forbes. https://www.forbes.com/sites/darrahbrustein/2017/11/19/the-55-best-questions-to-ask-to-break-the-ice-and-really-get-to-know-someone/

Buskist, W., & Saville, B. K. (2019). *Creating rapport in the classroom.* Socialpsychology.org. https://www.socialpsychology.org/rapport.htm

Castrillon, C. (2021). *How to handle difficult conversations at work.* Forbes. https://www.forbes.com/sites/carolinecastrillon/2021/10/24/how-to-handle-difficult-conversations-at-work/

Centers for Disease Control and Prevention. (2021). *Tips for having a meaningful conversation | How Right Now.* Www.cdc.gov. https://www.cdc.gov/howrightnow/resources/tips-for-having-a-meaningful-conversation/index.html

Chen, A. (2020). *48 fear of public speaking statistics you should know in 2020.* Orai. https://orai.com/blog/fear-of-public-speaking-statistics/

Cheng, J. T., Tracy, J. L., Foulsham, T., Kingstone, A., & Henrich, J. (2013). Two ways to the top: Evidence that dominance and prestige are distinct yet viable avenues to social rank and influence. *Journal of Personality and Social Psychology*, *104*(1), 103–125. https://doi.org/10.1037/a0030398

Cherry, K. (2022). *Starting a conversation when you are socially anxious*. Verywell Mind. https://www.verywellmind.com/how-to-start-a-conversation-4582339

Confidence. 2023. In *Oxford Dictionary*. Retrieved May 22, 2023, from https://www.oed.com/

Chow, W. S., & Chan, L. S. (2008). Social network, social trust and shared goals in organizational knowledge sharing. *Information & Management*, *45*(7), 458–465. https://doi.org/10.1016/j.im.2008.06.007

Choy, E. (2020). *10 ways to use storytelling in the workplace every day*. Www.linkedin.com. https://www.linkedin.com/pulse/10-ways-use-storytelling-workplace-every-day-esther-choy

Cohen, B., & Silver, S. (1989). *Introduction to a theory of group structure and information exchange**. https://core.ac.uk/download/pdf/147255045.pdf

Cote, C. (2020). *How to create an effective value proposition | HBS Online*. Business Insights - Blog. https://online.hbs.edu/blog/post/creating-a-value-proposition

Council, F. C. (2017). *Council post: 14 ways to be more mindful of how you speak to employees*. Forbes. https://www.forbes.com/sites/forbescoachescouncil/2017/05/01/14-ways-to-be-more-mindful-of-how-you-speak-to-employees/

Dunbar, R. I. M. (2017). Breaking Bread: the functions of social eating. *Adaptive Human Behavior and Physiology*, *3*(3), 198–211. https://doi.org/10.1007/s40750-017-0061-4

Economy, P. (2020). *7 tips for making socializing much less painful for introverts who need to network.* Inc.com. https://www.inc.com/peter-economy/7-tips-for-making-socializing-much-less-painful-for-introverts-who-need-to-network.html

Forgas, J. P. (2011). She just does not look like a philosopher…? Affective influences on the halo effect in impression formation. *European Journal of Social Psychology, 41*(7), 812–817. https://doi.org/10.1002/ejsp.842

Forsey, C. (2020). *What you need to know about commercial use.* Blog.hubspot.com. https://blog.hubspot.com/marketing/commercial-use#:~:text=What%20is%20commercial%20use%3F

Fryer, B. (2014). *Storytelling that moves people.* Harvard Business Review. https://hbr.org/2003/06/storytelling-that-moves-people

Gallo, A. (2017). *How to keep your team focused and productive during uncertain times.* Harvard Business Review. https://hbr.org/2017/03/how-to-keep-your-team-focused-and-productive-during-uncertain-times

Gilron, R., & Gutchess, A. H. (2011). Remembering first impressions: Effects of intentionality and diagnosticity on subsequent memory. *Cognitive, Affective, & Behavioral Neuroscience, 12*(1), 85–98. https://doi.org/10.3758/s13415-011-0074-6

Glicksman, E., & Glicksman, E. (2022). *Jargon: It creates a wall between managers and employees.* SHRM. https://www.shrm.org/resourcesandtools/hr-topics/people-managers/pages/jargon-corporate-speak-business-lingo.aspx

Govil, S. (2018). *Everyone is talking about the future of work. Here are 4 ways to take your company into the future now.* Entrepreneur. https://www.entrepreneur.com/science-technology/everyone-is-talking-about-the-future-of-work-here-are-4/323348

Grenny, J. (2017). *Great storytelling connects employees to their work.* Harvard Business Review. https://hbr.org/2017/09/great-storytelling-connects-employees-to-their-work

Grenny, J. (2019). *4 things to do before a tough conversation.* Harvard Business Review. https://hbr.org/2019/01/4-things-to-do-before-a-tough-conversation

Hall, J. (2013). *13 simple ways you can have more meaningful conversations.* Forbes. https://www.forbes.com/sites/johnhall/2013/08/18/13-simple-ways-you-can-have-more-meaningful-conversations/

Han, S. (2021). *You can only maintain so many close friendships.* The Atlantic. https://www.theatlantic.com/family/archive/2021/05/robin-dunbar-explains-circles-friendship-dunbars-number/618931/

Harter, J., & Rigoni, B. (2015). *State of the american manager.* Gallup.com; Gallup. https://www.gallup.com/services/182138/state-american-manager.aspx

Hillsberg, C. (2021). *5 techniques to build rapport with your colleagues.* Harvard Business Review. https://hbr.org/2021/09/5-techniques-to-build-rapport-with-your-colleagues

Huberman, A. (2021). *Huberman Lab* (No. 11). Spotify. https://open.spotify.com/episode/7lR4jC90jef8ivbXE-fOdYP?si=d959f2f71e104375

Inabo, S. (2022). *What is customer rapport? (+8 ways to build it).* Zendesk. https://www.zendesk.com/blog/customer-rapport/

Indeed Editorial Team. (2022). *11 tips for communicating effectively with employees.* Indeed Career Guide. https://www.indeed.com/

career-advice/career-development/communicating-effectively-with-employees

Intuit Mailchimp. (n.d.). *Business value proposition: How to write & importance*. Mailchimp. Retrieved May 21, 2023, from https://mailchimp.com/resources/value-proposition-writing/

Jerome, G. (2011). *How to break the ice and meet new people*. Reader's Digest. https://www.rd.com/article/how-to-break-the-ice-and-meet-new-people/#:~:text=Break%20the%20ice%20by%20making

Khan Academy. (2016). *What are social groups and social networks?* Khan Academy. https://www.khanacademy.org/test-prep/mcat/society-and-culture/social-structures/a/what-are-social-groups-and-social-networks

Kitterman, T. (2023). *How employee storytelling helps build empathy at work*. Great Place to Work®. https://www.greatplacetowork.com/resources/blog/how-employee-storytelling-helps-build-empathy-at-work

Knight, R. (2020). *How to talk to your team when the future is uncertain*. Harvard Business Review. https://hbr.org/2020/04/how-to-talk-to-your-team-when-the-future-is-uncertain

Kory Westlund, J. M., & Breazeal, C. L. (2019). A long-term study of young children's rapport, social emulation, and language learning with a peer-like robot playmate in preschool. *Frontiers*. https://dspace.mit.edu/handle/1721.1/123871

Lebowitz, S. (2019). *14 ways to skip shallow small talk and have deep conversations*. Business Insider. https://www.businessinsider.com/how-to-skip-small-talk-and-have-deep-conversations-2015-12

Library, J., & Wilson, A. (2005). *CSUSB ScholarWorks CSUSB ScholarWorks Theses Digitization Project First impressions through the constructs of impression First impressions through the constructs of impression management management.* https://scholarworks.lib.csusb.edu/cgi/viewcontent.cgi?article=3764&context=etd-project

Lickerman, A. (2010). *The importance of tone.* Psychology Today. https://www.psychologytoday.com/us/blog/happiness-in-world/201008/the-importance-tone

Ligato, L. (2015). *The 5 best ways to break the ice on a dating app.* HuffPost. https://www.huffpost.com/entry/dating-apps-tips-tricks_n_5602baa4e4b08820d91af102

LinkedIn Social Entrepreneurship. (n.d.). *How do you use your social value proposition to inspire and engage your community and supporters?* Www.linkedin.com. Retrieved May 21, 2023, from https://www.linkedin.com/advice/0/how-do-you-use-your-social-value-proposition

Lipoff, S. (2015). *40 great conversation starters to break the ice.* Business Insider. https://www.businessinsider.com/great-conversation-starters-to-break-the-ice-2015-2

Lucena, G. (2020). *8 ways you can improve your persuasive communication skills.* General Intelligences. https://generalintelligences.org/2020/08/22/8-ways-you-can-improve-your-persuasive-communication-skills/

MacPherson, A. C., & Howard, P. W. (2011). *Group structure - an overview | ScienceDirect Topics.* Www.sciencedirect.com. https://www.sciencedirect.com/topics/psychology/group-structure#:~:text=Group%20structure%20has%20been%20defined

Mandel, E. (2021). *How to be social again: 5 post-pandemic socialization tips.* Scrubbing in by BSWHealth. https://www.bswhealth.com/blog/how-to-be-social-again-5-post-pandemic-socialization-tips

MasterClass. (2021). *How to write a fable in 5 steps.* MasterClass. https://www.masterclass.com/articles/how-to-write-a-fable-in-5-steps

MasterClass Staff. (2021). *How to build rapport: 6 tips for connecting with others.* MasterClass. https://www.masterclass.com/articles/how-to-build-rapport

McCann, J. (2014). *4 ways to talk to employees so they listen.* Entrepreneur. https://www.entrepreneur.com/article/232261

Mind Tools Content Team. (2023). *Building rapport.* Www.mindtools.com. https://www.mindtools.com/a9f9kqi/building-rapport

Moran, K. (2016). *The four dimensions of tone of voice.* Nielsen Norman Group. https://www.nngroup.com/articles/tone-of-voice-dimensions/

Mortensen, M., & Edmondson, A. C. (2023). *Rethink your employee value proposition.* Harvard Business Review. https://hbr.org/2023/01/rethink-your-employee-value-proposition

Mrkonjić, E. (2022). *Zoom statistics 2023: How video conferencing changed.* TeamStage. https://teamstage.io/zoom-statistics/#:~:text=According%20to%20various%20Zoom%20usage

North, M. (2020). *10 tips for improving your public speaking skills.* Professional Development | Harvard DCE. https://professional.dce.harvard.edu/blog/10-tips-for-improving-your-public-speaking-skills/

O'Corry-Crowe, G., Suydam, R., Quakenbush, L., Smith, T. G., Lydersen, C., Kovacs, K. M., Orr, J., Harwood, L., Litovka, D., & Ferrer, T. (2020). Group structure and kinship in beluga whale societies. *Scientific Reports, 10*(1), 11462. https://doi.org/10.1038/s41598-020-67314-w

Okten, I. O. (2018). Studying first impressions: What to consider? *APS Observer, 31*(2). https://www.psychological-science.org/observer/studying-first-impressions-what-to-consider

Parekh, D. (2019). *Council post: Communicate your point of view through storytelling.* Forbes. https://www.forbes.com/sites/forbescoachescouncil/2019/10/14/communicate-your-point-of-view-through-storytelling/

Pellicano, M. (2017). *4 essential types of tone of voice in communication.* Maria Pellicano. https://mariapellicano.com/four-types-tone-of-voice-in-communication/

Pellicano, M. (2018). *What is voice tone in communication.* Maria Pellicano. https://mariapellicano.com/what-is-tone-of-voice-in-communication/

Petersen, L. (2013). *How to deal with subordinates who refuse to respect you.* Chron.com. https://smallbusiness.chron.com/deal-subordinates-refuse-respect-69938.html

PLAINlanuage.gov. (n.d.). *plainlanguage.gov | Avoid jargon.* Www.plainlanguage.gov. https://www.plainlanguage.gov/guidelines/words/avoid-jargon/#:~:text=Special%20terms%20can%20be%20useful

Powers, K. W., & Diaz, J. B. B. (2022). What employees want most in uncertain times. *MIT Sloan Management Review, 64*(2). https://sloanreview.mit.edu/article/what-employees-want-

most-in-
uncertain-times/

Ricard, S. (2020). *Council post: Five strategies to improve communication with team members.* Forbes. https://www.forbes.com/sites/forbes-techcouncil/2020/01/08/five-strategies-to-improve-communi-cation-with-team-members/

Richards, D. (2014). Apathetic miscommunica-tion. *The seven sins of innovation,* 124–133. https://doi.org/10.1057/9781137432537_10

Robson, D. (2021a). *The conversational habits that build better connec-tions.* Www.bbc.com. https://www.bbc.com/worklife/arti-cle/20211109-what-we-get-wrong-about-conversations

Robson, D. (2021b). *Why you make better first impressions than you think.* Www.bbc.com. https://www.bbc.com/worklife/arti-cle/20210929-how-the-liking-gap-fuels-social-anxiety

Rosh, L., & Offermann, L. (2013). *Be yourself, but carefully.* Harvard Business Review. https://hbr.org/2013/10/be-yourself-but-carefully

Rowh, M. (2012, November). First impressions count. *Https://Www.apa.org.* https://www.apa.org/gradpsych/2012/11/first-impressions

Russo, M. D. (2018). *29 ways to break the ice IRL.* Www.refinery29.com. https://www.refinery29.com/en-us/conversation-starters-icebreaker-questions

Rutherford, O. (2020). *How to make friends with uber drivers part 2.* Medium. https://oliverkouroshrutherford.medium.com/how-to-make-friends-with-uber-drivers-part-2-431d389c61ba?source=user_profile---------2----------------------------

Schulz, J. (2017). *Using a person's name in conversation.* MSU Extension. https://www.canr.msu.edu/news/using_a_persons_name_in_conversation#:~:text=As%20much%20as%20we%20like

Shellenbarger, S. (2016). *Use Mirroring to Connect With Others.* WSJ; Wall Street Journal. https://www.wsj.com/articles/use-mirroring-to-connect-with-others-1474394329

Shortsleeve, C. (2018). *How to Make the Best First Impression, According to Experts.* Time; Time. https://time.com/5374799/best-first-impression-experts/

Siliezar, J. (2021). *Researchers Find Conversations Do not End When People Want Them To.* Harvard Gazette. https://news.harvard.edu/gazette/story/2021/03/researchers-find-conversations-dont-end-when-people-want-them-to/

Skydive Danielson. (2019). *5 Reasons Why People Skydive.* Www.skydivedanielson.com. https://www.skydivedanielson.com/why-do-people-skydive/

Smirnov, I., & Thurner, S. (2017). Formation of Homophily in Academic Performance: Students Change Their Friends Rather Than Performance. *PLOS ONE, 12*(8), e0183473. https://doi.org/10.1371/journal.pone.0183473

Staley, K. (2015). *30 Ways to Manage Speaking Anxiety | University Counseling Service - The University of Iowa.* Counseling.uiowa.edu. https://counseling.uiowa.edu/news/2015/09/30-ways-manage-speaking-anxiety

Steber, C. (2016). *11 Tips for Making Socializing Easier if You are an Introvert.* Bustle. https://www.bustle.com/articles/173730-11-tips-for-making-socializing-easier-if-youre-an-introvert

Steinhorst, C. (2021). *A Leader's Guide to Managing Employee Uncertainty*. Forbes. https://www.forbes.com/sites/curtsteinhorst/2021/06/16/a-leaders-guide-to-managing-employee-uncertainty/

Sundin, A., Andersson, K., & Watt, R. (2018). Rethinking Communication: Integrating Storytelling for Increased Stakeholder Engagement in Environmental Evidence Synthesis. *Environmental Evidence, 7*(1). https://doi.org/10.1186/s13750-018-0116-4

Taras, V., Shah, G., Gunkel, M., & Tavoletti, E. (2020). *Graduates of Elite Universities Get Paid More. Do They Perform Better?* Harvard Business Review. https://hbr.org/2020/09/graduates-of-elite-universities-get-paid-more-do-they-perform-better

Thacker, M. (2019). *Council Post: How to Create a Successful Value Proposition*. Forbes. https://www.forbes.com/sites/forbescoachescouncil/2019/07/15/how-to-create-a-successful-value-proposition/

The Decision lab. (2022). *Halo effect - Biases & Heuristics | The Decision Lab*. The Decision Lab. https://thedecisionlab.com/biases/halo-effect

The Economist. (2009). *The Halo Effect*. The Economist. https://www.economist.com/news/2009/10/14/the-halo-effect

Thompson, S. (2021). *12 Tips to Spark More Meaningful, Authentic Conversations*. Scrubbing in by BSWHealth. https://www.bswhealth.com/blog/12-tips-to-spark-more-meaningful-authentic-conversations

Tools for Clear Speech. (n.d.). *Style & Tone.* Tfcs.baruch.cuny. edu. https://tfcs.baruch.cuny.edu/style-tone/

Toteja, M. (2022). *Council Post: Five Keys to Effective Storytelling at Work.* Forbes. https://www.forbes.com/sites/forbes-coachescouncil/2022/03/01/five-keys-to-effective-storytelling-at-work/

Tran, C. (2015). *Are You Guilty of Having One-Way Conversations?* Www.linkedin.com. https://www.linkedin.com/pulse/you-guilty-having-one-way-conversations-christine-tran/

Travis, M. W. (2011). *What Is a Story, and Where Does It Come From?* TheWrap. https://www.thewrap.com/what-story-and-where-does-it-come-32636/

Tsipursky, D. G. (2023). *Building Trust and Rapport: 3 Social Intelligence Secrets for Better Stakeholder Relationships.* Forbes. https://www.forbes.com/sites/glebtsipursky/2023/04/30/building-trust-and-rapport-3-social-intelligence-secrets-for-better-stakeholder-relationships/

Turner, M. (n.d.). *Eden Blog | 5 Ways That Storytelling Can Improve Workplace Communication.* Www.edenworkplace.com. https://www.edenworkplace.com/blog/storytelling-workplace-communication

Twin, A. (2022). *Value Proposition.* Investopedia. https://www.investopedia.com/terms/v/valueproposition.asp

University of Colorado, Boulder. (n.d.). *Working on Yourself: How to Prepare for a Difficult Conversation.* Retrieved May 22, 2023, from https://www.colorado.edu/oiec/node/309/attachment

University of Minnesota. (2015). *2.1 The Value Proposition.* Open. lib.umn.edu; University of Minnesota Libraries Publishing

edition, 2015. This edition adapted from a work originally produced in 2010 by a publisher who has requested that it not receive attribution. https://open.lib.umn.edu/principlesmarketing/
chapter/2-1-the-value-proposition/

University of Minnesota. (2016a). *11.4 Persuasive Strategies*. Umn. edu; University of Minnesota Libraries Publishing edition, 2016. This edition adapted from a work originally produced in 2013 by a publisher who has requested that it not receive attribution. https://open.lib.umn.edu/communication/chapter/11-4-persuasive-
strategies/

University of Minnesota. (2016b). *13.1 Understanding Small Groups*. Open.lib.umn.edu; University of Minnesota Libraries Publishing edition, 2016. This edition adapted from a work originally produced in 2013 by a publisher who has requested that it not receive attribution. https://open.lib.umn.edu/communication/chapter/
13-1-understanding-small-groups/

University of New South Wales. (n.d.). *10 Tips for Speaking to an Audience*. Www.student.unsw.edu.au. https://www.student.unsw.edu.au/speaking-audience

University of Oxford. (2017). *Social Eating Connects Communities | University of Oxford*. Www.ox.ac.uk. https://www.ox.ac.uk/news/2017-03-16-social-eating-connects-communities

University of Pittsburgh. (n.d.). *Persuasive speaking | Department of Communication | University of Pittsburgh*. Www.comm.pitt.edu. https://www.comm.pitt.edu/persuasive-speaking

Small Talk [5 in 1]

University of Pittsburgh | Department of Communication. (n.d.). *Communication behaviors for effective small group work | Department of Communication | University of Pittsburgh.* Www.comm.pitt. edu. https://www.comm.pitt.edu/communication-behaviors-effective-small-group-work

University of Waterloo. (n.d.). *Teamwork Skills: Being an Effective Group Member | Centre for Teaching Excellence.* Uwaterloo.ca. https://uwaterloo.ca/centre-for-teaching-excellence/catalogs/tip-sheets/teamwork-skills-being-effective-group-member

Walia, C. (2020). *A Guide to Speaking in Front of a Crowd.* Www. linkedin.com. https://www.linkedin.com/pulse/guide-speaking-front-crowd-chetan-walia

Walle, E. A., & Campos, J. J. (2014). *APA PsycNet.* Psycnet.apa. org. https://psycnet.apa.org/record/2014-04652-001

Webster, J. G., & Ksiazek, T. B. (2012). The Dynamics of Audience Fragmentation: Public Attention in an Age of Digital Media. *Journal of Communication, 62*(1), 39–56. https://doi.org/10.1111/j.1460-2466.2011.01616.x

Westfall, C. (2021). *How to Keep a Conversation Going: 10 Ways to Connect and Engage With Anyone, Anywhere.* Forbes. https://www.forbes.com/sites/chriswestfall/2021/03/12/how-to-keep-a-conversation-going-10-ways-to-connect-and-engage-with-anyone-anywhere/

Whitler, K. A. (2014). *Why Word of Mouth Marketing is the Most Important Social Media.* Forbes. https://www.forbes.com/sites/kimberlywhitler/2014/07/17/why-word-of-mouth-marketing-is-the-most-important-social-media/?sh=25a52ab454a8

170

Zebrowitz, L. A., & Franklin, R. G. (2014). The Attractiveness Halo Effect and the Babyface Stereotype in Older and Younger Adults: Similarities, Own-age Accentuation, and Older Adult Positivity Effects. *Experimental Aging Research*, *40*(3), 375–393. https://doi.org/10.1080/0361073x.2014.897151

Exclusive Bonuses

Dear Reader,

I'm thrilled to introduce you to five incredible bonuses that will enhance your journey through the world of small talk and communication mastery. These bonuses are carefully crafted to complement the insights and strategies presented in our book, providing you with additional tools and resources to excel in your communication skills.

Bonus 1 - Conversational Mastery: A Guide to Practice and Improve Your Communication Skills

This bonus offers practical exercises and techniques to help you practice and enhance your communication skills. Dive deeper into the art of conversation, learn how to navigate various social situations, and develop confidence in your ability to connect with others.

Bonus 2 - Spark Your Conversations: A Guide to Engaging Conversation Starters

Never be at a loss for words again with this invaluable guide to conversation starters. Whether you're networking at a professional event or mingling at a social gathering, these conversation starters will help you break the ice and keep the conversation flowing effortlessly.

Bonus 3 - Reflect & Grow: A Journal of Self-Discovery and Reflection Self-reflection

This is a powerful tool for personal growth and development. Use this journal to reflect on your communication experiences, identify areas for improvement, and set goals for your journey towards becoming a better communicator.

Bonus 4 - Discover Your Voice: A Guide to Understanding Your Communication Style

Understanding your communication style is key to becoming a more effective communicator. This guide will help you uncover your unique voice, identify your strengths and weaknesses, and tailor your communication approach to better connect with others.

Bonus 5 - Converse & Conquer: Your Annual Conversation Challenge

Challenge yourself to level up your conversation skills with this year-long conversation challenge. Each month, you'll receive a new set of prompts and activities designed to push you out of your comfort zone and help you become a more confident and engaging communicator.

How to Access Your Bonuses:

Scan the QR Code Below: Simply use your phone's camera or a QR code reader to scan the code, and you'll be directed straight to the bonus content.

I hope you find these bonuses valuable additions to your journey towards mastering the art of small talk and communication.

Thank you for joining me on this exciting adventure, and here's to unlocking your full potential in the world of communication!

Warm regards,

Kirstin Rae Evans